Anointed Detectives

*Discerning the Voice of
God in our Every Day Lives*

Héctor Santos

Anointed Detectives by Héctor Santos

©2011 Hector Santos

ISBN 0-9665972-0-6

Cover design by: Adrian Franco.

Printed in the United States of America.

First edition.

Unless otherwise stated, biblical references are from the New King James Version. Used with permission. All italics and bolding of Scripture were included to highlight the emphasis of the author.

For more information please write to:
Hector Santos Ministries, Inc.
P.O. Box 17557
Rochester, New York 14621

Anointed Detectives: Discerning the Voice of God in our Every Day Lives

Table of Contents

Section 1: He Talks!

Section 11: Understanding the Puzzle Pieces

Section III: Organizing the Revelation (Doing a Detective's Work)

Endorsements

"Nothing is more important to God's Kingdom program in this present age than full equipping of the saints of God for the work of their ministry. That is as true for the prophetic as it is for the other four equipping offices and anointings. Hector Santos' book **"Anointed Detectives"** will serve as an effective resource for anyone desiring to see the prophetic more actively and accurately exercised in and through their lives."

Ronald A. Domina, Apostle
Lifenet Ministries International
Apostolic Oversight for Hector Santos Ministries

***

"The prophetic is perhaps one of the least understood and often misused gifts in the church today. Hector Santos has written a book that brings clarity and simplicity along with great understanding to this important topic. Written with humility and sprinkled with personal stories, humor and life applications, **"Anointed Detectives"** is an easy to read, how-to book for all who are seeking God for the prophetic in their lives."

Dave Branch, Senior Pastor
Faith Chapel of Churchville, NY

***

"I highly recommend **"Anointed Detectives"** as both a practical and valuable resource to help you begin or to further mature in receiving and communicating revelation from God with accuracy, clarity, right order and right character."

John R. Shoemaker, Senior Leader
Outlook Christian Center, Rochester, NY

Dedication &
Acknowledgements

This book is dedicated to my Lord and Savior, **Jesus Christ**!
Lord, You have redeemed me back to my Heavenly Father and
placed Your Holy Spirit within me. Then, You placed this call and passion
within me to prophetically equip the saints. I've written this book in
obedience to You! And it is to You that I lift up this work and declare:
May You receive all of the glory, may Your name be praised, and may
Your people be equipped to hear Your voice more than ever before.
Amen.

I could not have taken on such a project of writing this book without
a strong-dedicated team around me that provided much-needed support
and encouragement. I am truly grateful to the awesome people that God
surrounded me with. My heart is full of gratitude and I'd like to take this
opportunity to express my appreciation.

To my wife **Barbara (my Barbie)**…Honey thank you so much for
your support through this. Thank you for allowing me to hide myself in
prayer and to dedicate myself to writing. I couldn't have done this without
you. God has truly put a warrior by my side, and I am so grateful for you.
This is our victory! To my daughters, **Alyssa Rose** and **Leilani Marie**,
my two little prophets-in-training. You two have been heaven's gifts to my
life. Thank you for letting Daddy spend the time he needed writing even
though you wanted to play a game or go for a walk. The book is done!
Now we can catch up on our play time!!! I love you two with all of my
heart!

To my godly mother **Wilma Santos**… Mom, thanks for all of your
help throughout the writing of this book. By help, you know I mean for all
of your research help with Scriptures, editing, praying, and most important, for the example that you have set for me of trusting in the Lord.

Love you. To my Dad **Eugenio**…God has placed a passion for music within you and has made you a wonderful musician. Thanks for your example of how one must have passion for what he loves. By that example, I'm fulfilling my ministry "passionately"! To my brother **Carlos** and his lovely family…You are a man of great purpose. I look with anticipation for what's being developed in your life now. The world better get ready for your ministry! To my sister **Joann** and her great family…I'm grateful for your love for me. I've always known that I was protected by two forces: 1-the Lord and 2-my older sister! You have also provided an awesome example that living led by the Lord will always prosper you. To my brother **Luis**…God has put an anointing on your life as well. The Seer Anointing is just beginning to flow in you. You are also proof that we are truly a prophetic family. I also thank God for my late **Aunt Eufemia Escalera** who was an awesome example of living a lifestyle of prayer and who helped put a desire in me to experience God's supernatural power. To my incredible in-laws **Roberto & Abigail Nieves**…it's not true what they say about in-laws. You two have been awesome encouragers, cheering me on to fulfill my ministry. Thank you for your words of counsel and love. **Ivan & Chrisy Soto**…thanks for your support whenever we have to get away. Love you guys.

To my awesome pastors, **Apostle Ron & Karen Domina**. I am so grateful for your love for my family and me. I would not be fulfilling my ministry had it not been for your acknowledging the call in me and for giving me a place to grow and develop. I'm thrilled that we are Kingdom building together! Thanks for all of your help! To my church family, the congregation at **Bethel Christian Fellowship**…thank you for your support.

To my spiritual parents, **Pastor Benny & Sandy Thomas**. I would have to write a book to explain to the world how instrumental you were in me launching in ministry! By God's design our paths have crossed and now He has made us as "two families inside of one vehicle!" Thanks for your examples, counsel, and for all of the various forms of support you've assisted with. We love you guys!

To my Ministry Friends: **Pastor Dave & Pat Branch**…you are like family! Looking forward to working together more in the future. **Pastor John Shoemaker**…"mi amigo" who has been there for me. I'm grateful for you! To my ministry leaders at The Samuel Company School of Prophetic Equipping, and Pure Streams ministry…thank you for all of your help. How great it is to be surrounded by people with a passion for the prophetic! Thank you all for believing in me and my ministry.

To my friends: **Joaquín Peréz**…you have been an awesome armor bearer! We still have lots of work to do! **Natalia Byrd**…thank you for your hard work on editing this manuscript and for translating this book into Russian. We appreciate you "Simya"!

To the end-time army of Anointed Detectives…this book is for you. Rise up and hear the voice of your Master who is calling you to fulfill your destinies! The time is short and the laborers are few…and yet the harvest is ready. May the revelation in this book light a passion within you to hear from God in a new way, and may it cause you to take action to manifest the Kingdom of Heaven to the world around you. Let's be His prophetic army in the earth today!

Foreword

At last! A much needed writing on hearing from God in the end times. The practicality of a good detective at work is a perfect match with seeking and finding in order to see and hear God's ongoing communication. I believe this unique analogy in print is going to open the eyes and ears of many believers to a new and higher level of communion with God.

Having known Hector for many years, I can attest that his perpetual quest in life has been to continually hear from God. It is evident to me that he is the right man to write this book.

If you are a serious follower of Jesus Christ who wants all that God has for you, then I believe you will bond with these writings from the first chapter on. So, put on your detective's hat and step into the adventure of becoming ..."God's Anointed Detective!"

Benny Thomas
Benny Thomas Ministries
Beaumont, Texas

Preface

Why do I write and teach on the topic of God's voice? Simple – it's been my lifelong passion. It's true! I've always had a passion to learn to hear the voice of God in my life. I've always wanted to know what God had in store for me, and I'm thankful that He is a God that would share His plans with His children.

There have been many great books released throughout the years that deal with learning how to hear the voice of God. I thank God for the many teachers who have risen up in the body of Christ to give solid, biblical teaching on how to increase our hearing. These teachings have been foundational stones that have allowed us to learn how to be led by the Spirit of God.

This, however, is not just another book on learning how to hear the voice of God! You may be wondering, "I already have 10 books on my shelf that deal with this topic. Why read another one?" While this book does deal with the topic of hearing God's voice, it has another main purpose.

There has been an increase in receiving communication from God, over the years, however, I've continued to encounter a certain phenomena among believers – a lack of ability to receive confirmation that what God is speaking to them is accurate. As a result, believers are running around looking for someone else to validate their hearing. Part of the reason why there is a lack of confirmations is that most believers are only activated in 1 or 2 ways in which God speaks.

This book will deal with the topic of hearing the voice of God in ALL of the ways in which he speaks and how to organize revelation (God's voice) to see what He is saying to us. The Holy Spirit is seeking those who would be interested to become "Anointed Detectives" — a company of prophetic believers who are on the hunt for God. In the days in which we are living, we need to be a people that know how to hear from God and be open to receive from Him regardless of which method He uses to speak to us.

Let's get ready to sharpen our skills to not only hear from God, but also receive confirmations that He is speaking to us a sure word!

Section 1:

He Speaks!

-1-
God Speaks Today!

Did you know that God speaks today? Has anyone shared that great news with you? Not only is He communicating from heaven, He is communicating a lot! My whole identity as a prophetic believer is wrapped up in the fact that my God speaks to me on a daily basis. My getting to that point where I could hear from God with great frequency, however, was not instant.

My journey to learn how to hear the voice of God was like any journey that contained its highs and lows. I've had powerful encounters that have left me in awe of the God that we serve. I've also gone through my seasons of feeling rejected because "God was speaking to other people and not to me". I experienced the poison of jealousy rising within me as I would overhear great news of what God was doing in someone else's life. I would later repent of those emotions and would continue to seek the Lord.   My cry was continual, "God, I want to learn to hear Your voice, to know Your will and to obey."

While every journey has a destination, you cannot reach it until you embark from your starting point. Here's how it started for me.

An Early Introduction to God's Voice

I have to say that I was fortunate to have been raised in a home where we believed in a communicating God. We were a church-going family that would attend the house of the Lord multiple times in a week. It was at this Pentecostal church where I was trained up in the Bible and in my basic faith in God. However, it was at home where I learned that my relationship with God was not confined to my church attendance.

My earliest memories recall stories that my mother would tell us about the times she spent in prayer and how God would answer her. That fascinated me! *"God responded to you?"* I would ask my mom with a sense of excitement. I couldn't hear her answers; I'd get distracted staring into space trying to picture the exchange.

11

My childhood imagination would conjure up mental images of a powerful Being on a throne that would hear the prayers of a single mother and would throw a thunderbolt in her direction and "hit" her with the answer. I could also picture this Being speaking loudly through a golden trumpet, and His voice would cut through the air until it finally arrived at my humble home with my mother hearing its decree. Wow! I was thrilled at the idea. I found soon enough, however, that even though the concept was thrilling, this Being was not speaking to me.

I remember asking God to speak to me so that I could hear His voice. I wanted the same relationship that my mother had with Him – I yearned for it.

One other thing that I was grateful for was that my family held weekly devotions in the basement. Since there were no chairs, my uncle made little wooden benches for everyone. The basement became our family sanctuary where we would meet with God. We would start by singing worship songs. Then there were testimonies shared of what God was doing in our lives. The icing on the cake was when my mother or aunt would teach us from the Scriptures. Even though we were kids, there was a sense of God's presence that made us hunger for more of Him. Some of my fondest memories were during that time of my life.

A Fateful Encounter

One fateful Saturday afternoon, when I was around 8 years old, my mother and my aunt had to run some errands. Being that my aunt and her four kids lived in the apartment below us, it left eight of us trying to find something to do with ourselves. Half the group decided to go outside and play football, leaving the remaining half (myself included) searching for a pastime. Suddenly my sister had a brilliant suggestion. "Hey, let's have family devotions." It was settled; the group responded with great enthusiasm.

My oldest cousin immediately pulled rank and decided that she would be the "preacher" for the devotion. Then my sister decided she would be the "usher", which meant that while my cousin preached, she would walk around telling the rest of us to be quiet and to pay attention. I don't recall what message my cousin preached that day, but I was un-aware that I was about to have my first experience with the living God, which would mark my life forever.

As the devotions ended, we decided that we would form a circle to close in prayer. Just as I was about to pray, when I closed my eyes, I suddenly saw a hideous demonic face looking right at me. Ironically, I also noticed that we had transitioned from a prayer to dismiss the service to a prayer of rebuking the enemy. It was amazing! My sister and cousins had no idea what I was seeing, and yet they were praying and taking authority over the enemy. It was spiritual warfare at its finest!

The demonic face I saw was so scary that I opened my eyes and began to cry.

My sister Joann who was next to me said, "Hector, what's wrong?"

"I see a demon looking at me and I'm afraid of it," I responded.
"That's just the enemy trying to scare you. Rebuke him. Remember that you have power." Being that we grew up in a Pentecostal church, we were familiar with such prayers and were taught that we had authority over the enemy.

So with all of the courage that I could muster up as an 8 year old, I closed my eyes and confronted the demonic face that was still looking at me. It's as if I had to close my eyes to see into the spirit world. I began to rebuke. "Satan, I rebuke you in the name of Jesus." Immediately the ugly face left, but another one came in its place, then one after that and yet another one after that. I continued rebuking the ugly faces that were there to intimidate me.

These demonic faces looked like grisly Halloween masks. Some had knives protruding into their heads. Some faces had blood gushing out of their noses and eyes. There were many faces with long sharpened fangs. It was as if I was able to see the face of every member of a de-monic legion, one by one. It was horrible to say the least!

As the battle raged on, there were times that I would stop rebuking and would bury my teary face into my sister's arm telling her that I couldn't do it. With a military authority, she would order me not to give up but to keep fighting. Finally, after what seemed like hours, the last demonic face disappeared.

A Vision from Heaven

Without warning, I was suddenly immersed in a peace that was way beyond my understanding. I felt safe, secure, and in a state of perfect love. As I stood in that circle enjoying the moment of feeling God's love washing all over me, I saw a vision. It surprised me! Prior to this occasion I've never seen a vision – I didn't even know what a vision was!

I noticed a difference with this vision. When I saw the demonic faces, although I saw them clearly, they were in a drab, grayish color. In contrast, this vision was detailed, VIVID and in full color.

A giant screen opened up before me, and I saw three pictures flash on the screen as a slideshow. In the first picture I saw a beautiful, golden clock. In the second picture I saw a bridge. Then in the last picture, I saw a dark woman walking with a basket on her head in a poor village scattered with straw huts. It looked like something you would see in Africa.

After I saw the vision, I opened my eyes to see my sister and cousins looking at me strangely. Apparently they had already finished praying for a while already and were wondering why I was standing there with my eyes closed. I shared the vision with them. We pondered it for a moment, and then we went out to play. However, from that moment on, there was an increase of hearing the voice of God in dreams and other ways that He would speak to me.

It wasn't until years later that I learned the full meaning of what occurred on that day. God was showing me by His Spirit that He had a plan for my life, and that even though I would have to battle through demonic attacks (the demonic faces), He would ultimately give me the victory. Then He was showing me that in His time (clock) I would be transitioning into God's plan for my life, and the end result would be that I would be sent by Him (bridge) to minister the Word of the Lord to people from even the most remote places on earth (dark woman in poor village).

That is exactly what has taken place in my life. After receiving that revelation, I went through some very dark times in my life as a teenager and rebelled on all levels. I rededicated my life to Christ when I was 16, but many of the struggles continued for years. Now, close to 30 years from when I had the vision, I am seeing the result of walking into God's plan for my life. I am enjoying a powerful relationship with God the Father. In His grace and mercy He has removed the shame from my youth and has given me a new identity. Praise God! Now ordained in the ministry, I have traveled to nations and continue to plan to do so as God leads. I'm seeing His plan for me unfolding with every approaching year.

A Recent Reminder

At the start of 2008, I received an invitation from a Pastor friend to come to his church to meet a Prophet who would be ministering there. I went more to see if there would be a ministry connection with the traveling minister. I didn't expect to receive a word and even less, receive one that would mean so much to me.

The weekend prior to having received this invitation, I was revisiting the vision that I saw when I was a kid. I was pondering it in my heart and was telling my wife that I wasn't sure if I had interpreted the vision correctly. I wasn't sure about the bridge and the lady in the poor village that I saw in that vision. Did it mean that I would transition geographically to Africa? I was hoping it wasn't so because I didn't feel called to Africa. My wife just very wisely responded, "Honey, let's let God show us."

The following Sunday, I took my family to my Pastor friend's church to hear the Prophet preach. At one point during the sermon, however, he slowly began to make his way up the aisle and toward us. Finally, he arrived at our pew and looking right at us, unloaded a powerful prophetic word over us regarding God's plans for our ministry. Just as he was closing, he pointed to me and said, "The Lord says to you that He is building a solid **bridge** for you into many

nations. You can be sure that it is a solid **bridge** that He is building for you and it will be a **bridge** so that you could go **into nations and come out of nations**." Amen.

That ministered to me so much because I was just having a sense in my spirit that God wanted to clarify to me the meaning of the vision. Being that I have activated myself to hear from God in the many ways that He speaks, I wasn't surprised that He in fact sent me to my friend's church to receive the much-needed clarification. I now understood that I would go into and out of nations. God spoke to me through a prophet to confirm and clarify what He had spoken to me directly many years prior.

A Communicating God

I am so grateful that we serve a communicating God! Hallelujah! Could you imagine if God were not a Communicator? What would that be like? How would we have intimacy with Him? Even on this earth we know that any relationship worth keeping will require good communication. Can you imagine God not talking with you? Just imagining that void should make us realize what a pleasure it is to hear from God.

During the time of King Ahab in the Old Testament, there was one prophet who was used mightily by God – Elijah. In 1 Kings 18, prophet Elijah challenged the false prophets of Baal to a duel on Mount Carmel. What was the issue that they were trying to prove? They wanted to prove which God was the true God; Jehovah or Baal. According to the challenge, the real living God would respond from heaven with fire! Elijah was cordial enough that he even let the "Baalers" go first. After much time and many rituals, there was no fire being sent from heaven. I love how the prophet Elijah began to taunt them.

> *So they took the bull which was given them, and they prepared it, and called on the name of Baal from morning even till noon, saying, "O Baal, hear us!" But there was no voice; no one answered. Then they leaped about the altar which they had made. And so it was, at noon, that **Elijah mocked them and said, "Cry aloud, for he is a god; either he is meditating, or he is busy, or he is on a journey, or perhaps he is sleeping and must be awakened."** So*

they cried aloud, and cut themselves, as was their custom, with knives and lances, until the blood gushed out on them. And when midday was past, they prophesied until the time of the offering of the evening sacrifice. ***But there was no voice; no one answered, no one paid attention.***
1 Kings 18:26-29 (emphasis mine)

Now, the false prophets of Baal knew what it felt like to not have anyone listen or pay attention to their clamors. I'm sure it wasn't a nice feeling to call out to heaven all day only to get no reply! Talk about rejection!

Elijah, on the other hand, was on the right team. He was on the team representing Jehovah – the communicating God! Here's what happened.

*Then Elijah said to all the people, "Come near to me." So all the people came near to him. And he repaired the altar of the LORD that was broken down. And Elijah took twelve stones, according to the number of the tribes of the sons of Jacob, to whom the word of the LORD had come, saying, "Israel shall be your name." Then with the stones he built an altar in the name of the LORD; and he made a trench around the altar large enough to hold two seahs of seed. And he put the wood in order, cut the bull in pieces, and laid it on the wood, and said, "Fill four waterpots with water, and pour it on the burnt sacrifice and on the wood." Then he said, "Do it a second time," and they did it a second time; and he said, "Do it a third time," and they did it a third time. So the water ran all around the altar; and he also filled the trench with water. And it came to pass, at the time of the offering of the evening sacrifice, that Elijah the prophet came near and said, "LORD God of Abraham, Isaac, and Israel, let it be known this day that You are God in Israel and I am Your servant, and that I have done all these things at Your word. Hear me, O LORD, hear me, that this people may know that You are the LORD God, and that You have turned their hearts back to You again." **Then the fire of the LORD fell and consumed the burnt sacrifice, and the wood and the stones and the dust, and it licked up the water that was in the trench. Now when all the people saw it, they fell on their faces; and they said, "The LORD, He is God! The LORD, He is God!"***
1 Kings 18:30-39 (emphasis mine)

God responded to Elijah! He responded by sending fire from

heaven! The end result was that a godless group of false prophets not only saw that there was a true living God, but they met their doom as well. As the story continues, Elijah takes action and demands that the false prophets be killed. What a powerful statement God was sending to Israel through this event! He was demonstrating to them that He was the only true God – and that He is to be revered.

Elijah had a relationship with God and was confident that He would communicate the much needed response on Mt. Carmel. I doubt that he would have gone into that challenge without a prior experience of hearing the voice of God. His faith in God's willingness to communicate led him to win that battle!

Guess what? Just as God responded to Elijah and many others throughout the Bible, God is still responding to His children today. He is a communicating God!

God's Plan for Intimacy

God created us for intimacy. He created us for relationship. In His wisdom, He gave us a free will so as not to force us to love and serve Him. While He extends His invitation for all mankind to enter into a relationship with Him, the choice is ours, and He will respect our decision. For those who enter into the relationship with the heavenly Father, like any other relationship, it includes regular communication.

In Genesis 2, we see that God forms Adam and breathes life into him so that he becomes a living being. In verse 16 it says that God commanded Adam which trees were okay to pick food from and which ones to avoid. You may think that it was harsh, but actually that communication was God's love toward His creation. In verse 19 it says that God brought the animals and beasts of the field to Adam so that Adam could name them. That communication was God's way of releasing man to have dominion over the animal kingdom. In verse 21 God fashioned woman out of Adam's rib. That communication was God's method of providing man with the necessary helpmate to both have dominion and to multiply. Throughout their being established in the Garden, God's continual guidance and insight was vital to their prosperity.

We do know that man rebelled and sinned and was dealt severe consequences for not obeying the voice of the Lord. Even in the process of being expelled from the garden, God didn't remove His communication completely.

In Genesis 3:8-22, God is dealing with Adam and Eve's disobedience. Verse 8 gives us a peek at what a normal day for Adam and Eve was like in the garden – they enjoyed sweet communion with God. It says that they heard the sound of the Lord walking in the garden in the cool of the day. Surely He was on His way to confront them, but look at what a beautiful closeness they shared with God that His walking in the Garden would be a normal occurrence in their day.

Then in Genesis 3:15, God tells the serpent, "And I will put enmity between you and the woman, and between your seed and her seed; He shall bruise you on the head, and you shall bruise his heel." With those words, God dealt the final blow to the one operating through the serpent – Satan. This piece of communication was God's way of letting Satan know that He was still in control and that He would provide a Redeemer who would once again reconcile man with God – Jesus Christ the Redeemer!

After the spiritual fall of mankind, God continued to communicate directly with His children to declare His intentions for their lives. God told Cain that He would put a mark on him to protect him from those wanting to kill him. Enoch walked so close with God that God just took him! God led Abram from Ur of the Chaldeans to Canaan and made him into the father of many nations. God led Noah to build an ark to save a remnant from destructive floods. Others led by God were Isaac, Jacob and Joseph – just to name a few.

A Shift in Communication

In the time of Moses, however, an event took place that shifted the way that God began to communicate with His people. After many years suffering the cruelty of slavery in a foreign land, the Hebrews cried out to God to deliver them. Responding to those prayers, God called Moses. After Moses was instructed by God to lead His people out of Egypt and into the wilderness, God was getting ready to present the people with a new form of government — a Theocracy. He was planning to introduce Himself! Up to that point only Moses and Aaron had heard the voice of the Lord. Now the people were receiving an invitation to meet the God who had delivered them.

> *"And the LORD said to Moses, 'Behold, I come to you in the thick cloud, that the people may hear when I speak with you, and believe you forever.' So Moses told the words of the people to the LORD. Then the LORD said to Moses, 'Go to the people and consecrate them today and tomorrow, and let them wash their clothes. And let them be ready for the third day. For on the third day the LORD will come down upon Mount Sinai in the sight of all the people. You shall set bounds for the people all around, saying: Take heed to yourselves that you do not go up to the mountain or touch its base. Whoever touches the mountain shall surely be put to death. Not a hand shall touch him, but he shall surely be stoned or shot with an arrow; whether man or beast, he shall not live. When the trumpet sounds long, they shall come near the mountain.' So Moses went down from the mountain to the people and sanctified the people, and they washed their clothes. And he said to the people, 'Be ready for the third day; do not come near your wives.'" Exodus 19:9-15*

After receiving this invitation, the people prepared themselves as per God's instructions. They were just as curious to see who the Being was that heard their cries in Egypt and was kind enough to deliver them. However, look at their reaction when it was time for the encounter.

> *"Now all the people witnessed the thunderings, the lightning flashes, the sound of the trumpet, and the mountain smoking; and when the people saw it, they trembled and stood afar off.* **Then they said to Moses, 'You speak with us, and we will hear; but let not God speak with us, lest we die.'** *And Moses said to the people, 'Do not fear; for God has come to test you, and that His fear may be before you, so that you may not sin.' So the people stood afar off, but Moses drew near the thick darkness where God was." Exodus 20:18-21 (emphasis mine)*

What happened? The people were not ready for an encounter with God. They had spent the years of their existence up to that point in an idolatrous country -Egypt. They placed their hope in the living God, but they did not know Him personally. Now, God was ready to meet with them directly, but they were afraid. Even Moses tried to get them to not fear and to take advantage of the opportunity to meet God – but they weren't having any of it! They told Moses, "We'll listen to you but don't let God speak to us or we'll die."

That event shifted the way God began to communicate with His children. From that point on, we see God raising up the prophets to serve as His mouthpiece to His people. Rather than God's original direct communication, now He began to speak His words to a middleman who would declare them to the people. There were some individuals who God spoke to directly after that point, but overall the people as a whole would hear from God through the prophet.

A Shift Back to the Original Plan

The story doesn't end there! When Jesus Christ died on the cross of Calvary, the Bible says that the veil separating The Holy Place from the Holy of Holies was rent in two. Only the High Priest had access to the Holy of Holies, which contained the presence of God. With that veil being torn, so was torn the old structure that we had to go through a middleman to get to God. Jesus restored our direct communication with God the Father.

As a matter of fact in John 10:27 Jesus says, "My sheep hear My voice, and I know them, and they follow Me." If you belong to Jesus, you can hear the voice of God, know Him intimately, and the end result is that you will be led by God in all areas of your life. What a beautiful promise!

God shifted back to His original plan to speak directly with His children. He further provided a help to us by giving us His Holy Spirit. Our bodies are now temples of the Holy Spirit, and God indwells our spirits through His Holy Spirit. Now God will continue to speak through prophets and prophecy as He did in the Old Testament. The difference is that now those methods of communication go hand in hand with what God is speaking to us directly as well.

A Communication Drought

There were times in the Bible when God wasn't speaking that often; there was a communication drought.

> "Now the boy Samuel ministered to the LORD before Eli. **And the word of the LORD was rare in those days;** *there was* **no widespread revelation**." 1 Samuel 3:1 (emphasis mine)

During that time, God wasn't talking all that much to His people. As we see from the Scriptures, they weren't all that great with following His instructions anyway, being that they were rebellious.

Also, from church history we know that between the book of Malachi in the Old Testament to the Gospel books of the New Testament, that there were 400 years. These years are referred to as the "silent years," in which God wasn't communicating all that often. The communication drought was suddenly interrupted in Luke 1. We see the window of heaven suddenly begin to open when the angel Gabriel tells Zacharias the priest that he's having a son – John the Baptist. Then we read about the young Mary who also hears from Gabriel that she will have a Son – Jesus. It is the beginning of the story of Jesus coming to redeem mankind.

Even though there were periods of silence from heaven, God would eventually begin to communicate again.

A Communication Boom

In our time, however, we don't have a problem with a heavenly silence. God is not only communicating, He is advancing His communication.

> *'And it shall come to pass in the last days, says God, That I will pour out of My Spirit on all flesh; Your sons and your daughters shall prophesy, Your young men shall see visions, Your old men shall dream dreams. And on My menservants and on My maidservants I will pour out My Spirit in those days; And they shall prophesy.'* Acts 2:17-18

We are living in those last days and a sign of that is exactly what God promised – increased communication! He also promised that we would see an increase of the gifts of the Holy Spirit in operation. We are living in the days of that promise being fulfilled. We must know Him intimately and learn how to hear His voice in all of the ways He speaks.

In the natural realm, communication is booming and exploding. I remember the days when we had 8-track tape players in our cars. If you liked a song, you had to keep on driving until it came up again. There was no reverse button. Then we moved on to cassettes, then CD's. Now we have the internet, email, fax machines, DVR, DVD, etc. Even teenagers and pre-teens all have their own cell phones and websites. Communication has increased so much that you may have an ongoing relationship with a friend and never hear their actual voice once! That is made possible with emails, text messages, chat rooms, instant messenger, etc.

Just as communication is booming in the natural realm, it is also booming in the spiritual realm. God is not only talking today, He is increasing His communication and is looking for a prophetic people who would train up their spiritual senses to hear His voice and receive His instruction.

What About You?

Again, God has shifted back to His original plan of direct communication with His children. Have you shifted? Have you come to a place in your life where you are doing your part to hear the voice of God? Have you made room in your life for God's input? Do you know how to hear from God? Are you willing to take the necessary steps to become more sensitive to His voice? Are you willing to abandon all of your other sources of information such as friends, family, your own knowledge, your emotions, the media, your boss, etc.?

These are good questions to ask ourselves because hearing from God today requires action from us. I don't know about you, but I don't want to hear the voice of God once in a while; I want to hear from Him daily.

Good news: there is more for the believer who desires more from God. If you have a strong desire to know that God is real in your life, you must train yourself to hear from Him in all the ways He speaks, or you will not see the increase.

-2 -
Why Speak More than One Way?

The Washing Machine Dream

When I was a new Christian, I remember that certain prophetic ministers would come to the church I attended and would call people out and give them strong prophetic words. I remember the excitement that I felt as people were being called to receive a message from God. *"Maybe I'll be next. Maybe God will have something to tell me."* These were my constant thoughts. However, I would always leave the church disappointed at not being called out.

After several occasions of this happening to me, I began to feel rejected by God. I would do my best to get over my disappointment but could not understand why God wouldn't want to speak to me that way. Over the years, I eventually thought that I was over the rejection and had matured beyond it. To hide my disappointment, I acted like it didn't bother me. *"Why do I need a prophet to give me a word anyway?"* I would tell myself. Little did I know that God was going to use a problem that I was having with my washing machine to talk to me about my heart's folly.

After marrying my wife Barbie, we located the house we wanted to purchase in Irondequoit, New York. As part of the deal, the former homeowner included his old washer and dryer for the grand price of $1.00. We thought it was a deal because it would save us the expense of buying these new appliances. However, not too long after the transaction, we realized why the washer was part of the so-called deal.

We noticed that once we started a load of laundry, almost like clock work, the clothes would bunch up to one side of the machine. Whenever that would happen, the washing machine would release a loud "BUZZZZZ" sound. That awful noise would cause us to have to go back to the basement where the machine was located, redistribute the clothes and press the start button again. On good days it would continue just fine. Other days, I had to go into intense spiritual warfare by laying hands (and feet) for that machine to start up again and quit "buzzing". That machine always tested our patience – to say the least!

Shortly after moving into our house, I noticed that the sense of rejection by God started creeping into my thoughts no matter how much I fought it. This started happening because there were decisions that I had to make, and I couldn't seem to get a clear answer from God. I could not get God to inspire anyone to prophesy to me or to bring me a solution to my problems. I was constantly complaining to God that other people got prophetic words from Him but I didn't. These "prayer times" were actually whining sessions where I would basically accuse God of having favorites and not liking me. Then one night during that period of my life, I had this dream:

> *I was in a school gymnasium with a large crowd of people. There was a guest prophetess who was going to prophesy over all of us. I was standing first in line and was very excited at the prospect of getting a prophetic word. Then the prophetess walks in, stands next to me and says, "God spoke to me and told me that I'm to start ministering at the other end of the line." So we all had to do an "about face" and instead of being first in line, I was now the last one. I was so upset at this new change of plans! As the prophetess began to minister at the other end of the line, I was very impatient for my turn. Finally, after ministering to many, she was now ministering to the person in front of me. I was very excited that I was next. Suddenly, just as the prophetess comes to lay hands on me to prophesy, I heard my washing machine "buzzing" in the basement of the school. So I told the prophetess, "Don't go anywhere. I just have to redistribute the clothes. I'll be right back." I ran to the basement of the school, redistributed the clothes, started the wash cycle again and when I got back upstairs, the light of the gymnasium was off and the prophetess was gone. I woke up.*

When I awoke, I could feel the waves of disappointment and rejection washing over me. I was furious, to say the least! I said, *"God, I can't get a prophetic word from You even in my dreams!"* My thoughts began to race, and I even contemplated that maybe I needed to hold back on my prayer time to show God how it felt like to be ignored. (And I thought I was a mature Christian then.) However, as I lay there plotting my revenge, the Holy Spirit began to speak to me ever so softly.

"Hector," He said, "examine the dream carefully. What were you wanting in the dream?"

"I wanted to hear from You through a prophetic word," I responded.

"Why does your washing machine make that buzzing noise?" He asked.

"Because all of the clothes are bunched up on one side."

"And what do you have to do to it?"

"I have to redistribute the clothes."

"Now, substitute 'bunched up' and 'redistribute' with the word balance."

"Okay, Lord, so the load of clothes in the washer gets unbalanced, and I have to balance it again so that the machine stops making the "buzzing" noise."

"Right! Likewise, so are you unbalanced when you look to hear from Me only through a prophet or a prophetic word. Just as you have to balance the clothes in the washer when you hear that noise, I want you to balance yourself because you're off balance. I want you to learn how to hear from Me for yourself and learn to hear from Me in all of the ways that I speak – not just one."

That was it! As the Holy Spirit showed me how the washing machine applied to my situation, everything else came together.

>   *Dream took place in a school = I was in a place of learning.

>   *The prophetess = prophets and the prophetic.

>   *The meeting was in the school's gymnasium = just as athletes train in a gym, I was being trained to walk in balance in hearing God's voice.

*The washing machine was in the school's basement and it was buzzing = just as a basement is the foundational slab of a structure, God was showing me that the foundational slab of God's communication is to learn to hear from God for myself. I was unbalanced because I wanted someone else to hear from God for me.

Now with this, I am not stating that God does not speak through prophets or the prophetic. What I am saying is that if we look to hear from God **only** through **one** of the ways He speaks, we are unbalanced and must renew our minds!

From that point of my life, everything changed. Not only did I buy a new washer (praise God), but my main priority was to learn how to hear the voice of God directly in all of the ways that He communicated. The process took years and it didn't lack its challenges, yet I don't regret surrendering myself to learning God's ways.

Today, my priority remains the same – to hear God's voice, obey Him and to do His will. My passion for hearing the voice of God continues…but this time without the disappointment. Now, because I have trained myself, not a day goes by that I don't hear God speak to me. I live in a constant place of communication and there is nothing better than *knowing* that you are exactly where God wants you to be.

Revelation Intervals

In my pursuit to hear from God, I have learned that God will give all believers the following levels of revelation: eternal, lifetime, seasonal, daily and *concealed*.

Let's define the various categories:

Eternal Revelation – In order for one to receive eternal revelation, one has to allow God to open the eyes of their understanding. Before, when we were lost in our sins, there were certain things about God that we had a hard time understanding and perceiving because the enemy blinded us.

> *"The god of this age has blinded the minds of unbelievers, so that they cannot see the light of the gospel of the glory of Christ, who is the image of God." 2 Corinthians 4:4*

The Holy Spirit, however, is very active today in His earthly out-reach to reveal eternal revelation to man. What eternal revelation? That Jesus Christ is the Savior of the world and the true Son of God! That God loves us with an everlasting love. That man can now be reconciled with God and we could live our lives with God by accept-ing what Jesus Christ did for us on the cross of Calvary. That for those who respond to the call, they will enjoy eternal life in the pres-ence of the Almighty God!

For the reason of salvation and redemption, the Father created us, the Son died for us and the Holy Spirit draws us. God's heart is to share this eternal revelation with every person on the terrestrial globe. We must pray for unbelievers that they will allow God to open the blinded eyes of their understanding to know Jesus Christ for who He is and enter the family of God.

Lifetime Revelation – It is very common for God to introduce Himself to someone and let them know early on what He intends for their life. These are a few examples from Scripture that support this theory:

Abraham – God told him he would be the father of many nations.

Noah – God told him that he would save his family from a great flood.

Joseph – God told him that he would be great and that His family would be under his authority.

Moses – God told him that he would deliver God's people out of Egypt and into "the land that flows with milk and honey."

Saul of Tarsus – God told Saul to go to Damascus. Then, it was revealed through the disciple Ananias that Saul would bear His name to the gentiles and to their kings and the people of Israel. God also said that Saul would be called to suffer for the sake of the Kingdom.

Just as God spoke to each of these individuals regarding their destinies, God continues to do so today. Through the various ways that He speaks, God will communicate to each believer and will reveal His plan for their destinies. When God formed us, He gave us differing gifts and talents to allow us to fulfill our callings. We all have that burning, innate question of *"Why am I here and what is my purpose?"* An answer only a loving Father can and will reveal!

Seasonal Revelation – With seasonal revelation, God speaks to us regarding the span of time that we are about to enter into. Seasons in God's timeframe may last days, weeks, months, years, or even decades. All we know is that our seasons are ordained by God to walk us into the full destiny He has for us. Each season contains challenges to strip away old things from our lives and blessings to encourage us to move forward out of that season and into the next one ahead.

There is a key word that must be stressed when we are talking about seasons – **transitions**! A transition is that place in between seasons. A transition takes place when you are walking out of the last season and are trying to identify what is next. It is usually in the place of transition when God will speak regarding the new season ahead of us. A word of caution: unless we have successfully completed the old season, God will allow us to repeat it until His purposes for that season are established. Therefore, let's cooperate with God and allow Him to complete and fulfill the work that He's started in us.

We find a great example of these "seasons" in Matthew 2:13. After Jesus was born, Herod was killing all of the babies 2 years and under. Joseph, the earthly father of Jesus, received a seasonal revelation in a dream. In the dream, the angel told Joseph to take Mary and the baby to Egypt to save Jesus from Herod. Joseph did! They were in Egypt for a season of a few years when Joseph received another message in a dream letting him know that it was time to go back to his hometown. Season by season, God led Joseph and his family to ensure the safety of the Son of God. God will also speak to us regarding our seasons for our safety and guidance.

Oh how I've had to trudge through some tough seasons. I remember a specific job that I knew God led me to, but I had no idea why. It wasn't too long before I despised going to work. I did not enjoy the type of work that I did or the people that I worked with. After complaining to God about my situation, He would just reply to me that it was His will for me to be there for a season. Well, that season lasted about 5 years. The great thing was that when the season ended, I realized that I had developed some wonderful managerial skills that I would not have developed anywhere else – skills that have helped me tremendously in my ministry. God led me there in that season of my life to sharpen me for my ministry call. So even if a seasonal call has you frustrated, be comforted by knowing that God has His purposes in it to bless and advance you.

Daily Revelation – In Exodus 16, we read that God provided manna for His people in the wilderness. However, He gave them strict instructions that they were to gather only enough for the day's need. Anything collected over that ration would rot and not be useful. Manna is symbolic of our daily provision that God wants to give us. Every day, God wants to feed us from His word to give us direction and affection for that day. God was giving His people a prophetic picture of what daily revelation looked like. Every day His people are to go to Him and collect the revelation needed for that day.

Now in the New Testament, we read about when Jesus was in the wilderness fasting and praying for 40 days and nights when Satan came to tempt Him. It says in Matthew 4 that Satan told Jesus, "*If you are the Son of God, command that these stones become bread.*" Jesus responded, "*Man shall not live by bread alone, but by every word that proceeds out of the mouth of God.*" Again, Jesus made that connection between earthly bread and heavenly bread (God's voice). Just as we need bread (food) to survive, we more importantly need "every word that proceeds out of the mouth of God". God provides daily communication for the believer who sets it in their heart to pursue it daily.

On this level of revelation, God speaks to us regarding all of the areas affecting our lives. He will talk to us about decisions we have to make. He will talk to us about areas of our lives that are still not surrendered to His majesty. He will talk to us about which contractor to hire to fix our roof. He will talk to us about where to get the car fixed to save 20% off of the bill. He will talk to us about how to create a better filing system that will make us more efficient at work. He will talk to us about the neighbor down the street that He wants us to go and share His heart with. God's daily revelation will deal with *every* area of our lives.

Concealed Revelation – God doesn't just hand over all revelation. To do so would be to spoil us. He's way too smart for that. In His infinite wisdom, God established that we would have to work to get some of His revelation. Concealed revelation is revelation that is acquired only when someone searches it out to uncover and discover it. There are some believers who enjoy hearing from God daily and seasonally but cannot go down deeper into the depths of God because they don't want to pay the price to uncover concealed revelation.

Proverbs 25:2 says, "It is the glory of God to conceal a matter, but the glory of kings is to search out a matter. You may ask yourself, *"Why in the world would God want to conceal something from me only to get me to find it? Why not just tell me?"* The answer to that question is received through the following Scripture.

> "But without faith it is impossible to please Him, for he that comes to God must believe that He is, **and that He is a rewarder of those who diligently seek Him.**" Hebrews 11:6 (emphasis mine)

God conceals revelation from us so that we could seek Him and receive a seeker's reward – revelation! Sure God could just show us something, but what would we gain if He has to constantly bring us everything we need? Remember, the Israelites had to go out in the wilderness and gather their daily manna. There are certain times when we want to hear from God on a matter and don't. I would say that God has concealed it so that you could go and search out His voice. If the answer doesn't come to you, don't stay by your mailbox, learn how to get up and uncover concealed revelation. God will hide from us the answer at times so that after we search it out, we will cherish that revelation due to the price of effort we paid for it.

It is interesting that the Lord will conceal a matter. Does He know us, or what? He knows how humans don't like to pay a price for anything. He knows that we don't want to work for anything. We usually want things free, we want them now and without strings attached. Our Heavenly Father is not interested in just dropping things onto our laps so that we could walk away from Him unappreciative. Remember, His goal is to draw us in deeper into Himself.

Another way to think about concealed revelation is like the child's game *Hide and Seek.* Let's say that you are praying to God and need an answer on something important. God heard your prayer and knows you are awaiting His response but knows that if it's just handed over, you'll miss His heart for you. So, He hides your answer by concealing it. Although your answer is established and released to you, it's released for you to seek it out. Remember what it says in Matthew 7:7, *"Ask, and it will be given to you; **seek, and you will find**, knock, and the door will be opened to you."* (emphasis mine) In order to unlock the answer, you must learn to do some seeking. We will go more into how to seek out a matter in later chapters.

"But what about deadlines? Why will God conceal a matter that I need answered so desperately?" Be at peace! God knows your deadlines. He knows by when you need to know what. Remember, however, that He responds to the prayer of faith. If you need to know soon, start praying in faith! Then trust in your heart and declare with your mouth that He holds all things in His hands and will respond in a timely manner.

In the following chapters, I will be referring only to seasonal, daily, and concealed revelation.

Paper Clues

When I was a kid, my sister and I broke open our piggy bank to order a children's album that we saw on a television infomercial. We ordered it and waited anxiously for it to arrive.

One day as we were arriving home from school, I noticed my older brother waiting for us at the front of the house. He said to us, "I have good news and bad news. The good news is that your album arrived in the mail today." My sister and I let out a loud "Hooray!" Then my brother says, "The bad news is that you'll have to find it." He then handed me a piece of paper that read, *"Look under your bed."*

My sister and I ran upstairs and looked under my bed. There was no album...just another piece of paper. That piece of paper read, "Now check in the refrigerator." We checked in the refrigerator and no album. The next sheet read, "Check outside by the tree." We went outside only to find another note. My brother had us running through the house like two tornadoes destroying everything in our path. Finally, the last clue led us to the album that brought us such joy during those years.

My brother Carlos always wanted to make the most fun out of everything. The pieces of paper were just another idea my brother had to make getting the album more interesting. God releases revelation to His children in a similar fashion.

Now God won't give us a 12-year download of all His guidance for us for that big time span. Rather, God will hand us a piece of revelation that will lead us to our next piece of revelation. Step by step, He will lead us along our way into our "promise land". As a result, we learn how to be led by the Spirit of God. Revelation from God will always lead you towards your destiny.

Some people may think, "Well, if God wants to talk to me, He can just talk to me." You're right; God can just talk to you. I guarantee you though, that if you are of that school of thought, you are missing much of God's communication towards you. If you want to hear Him more, open your mind to the thought that *you* have to make an effort to seek out what God wants to say to you.

Many Different Witnesses

2 Corinthians 13:1 says, *"By the mouth of two or three witnesses shall every word be established."* Why does God speak in so many different ways? So that we could have confirmations! God wants you not to only hear from Him, but to *know* that you've heard from Him. So every time He speaks something to you, He wants us to expect confirmations.

In the Old Testament, it was established in the law that nothing could be taken as authentic unless there were two or three witnesses. You couldn't bring an accusation against anyone, nor could a person be sentenced to death unless the lawful number of two or three witnesses testified against them. Paul referenced this law by repeating it in the book of 2 Corinthians. Being that it was a law that God had given His people, God also expects us to understand this important principle – God will repeat what He is saying to us. Even when Joseph interpreted the dream for Pharaoh that saved Egypt from a famine, Joseph mentioned to him, *"and the dream was re-peated to Pharaoh twice because the thing is established by God, and God will shortly bring it to pass."* Genesis 41:32

Look at it this way: when God speaks to you about direction for your life, you have received 1 witness. You cannot move on that direction unless you have the necessary 2 or 3 witnesses to make a case out of the revelation you have received. As you continue to wait on God, He will speak *other* ways to provide you the necessary witnesses. By understanding this form of guidance, we provide a safety net that would prevent presumption and save us unnecessary heartache.

I've heard cases of certain people who have received prophetic words that they were supposed to move geographically. After mov-ing to a new state and after many problems later, they have realized that they moved in presumption. Why? Because they didn't have the wisdom to allow God to continue to provide them with other "witnesses" that would support and confirm not only this revelation, but the timeline as well. When God sends you direction for your life, He knows how important it is to confirm that direction. The responsi-bility to confirm is God's – the responsibility to ask and watch for confirmations is ours. May we learn to walk wisely as we seek God for direction in our lives.

Puzzle Pieces

Now we know that God speaks in many different ways. Let's compare each way that God speaks as a piece of God's communi-cation puzzle.

When you buy a puzzle, there will usually be a picture of that puzzle on the top of the box. The answer that you need from God is like the picture on the top of the box – it is complete. As we pray and ask for God's input, just like how my brother gave me clues on pieces of paper, God begins to speak to you in different ways, which are like the puzzle pieces. Each time that God speaks to you in a different way about your prayer request, it is like receiving 1 puzzle piece to complete the puzzle. Our job is to continue listening for God and to receive those puzzle pieces in order to put them together and get a clear picture of what God is saying. The end result is a complete puzzle with all of the pieces, showing us a clear picture of what God is saying.

Could you get a clear picture of a puzzle with only 1 puzzle piece on the mat? Of course not! Yet many people launch out with only 1 piece of God's communication. We must learn to receive confirmations.

Train Yourself to Hear from God

As believers we need to train ourselves up in all of the ways God speaks. It's a skill that must be developed. All skills take time, effort and discipline to develop.

The first time my church invited me to preach, I preached under an open heaven for all of 5 minutes. After those 5 minutes were over, the heavy-iron door of heaven slammed shut, and I stood there speechless. The next time I preached I lasted 10 minutes. Today, I am an avid communicator and have to make sure that I have a time limit or I can easily go too long.

I want to encourage you to activate your senses to hear from God in all of the ways that He speaks. Don't fall into that place of ignorance that says God only talks to you certain ways. He only talks to you in those ways because those are the only ways you are aware that He talks. Read through the next chapters to learn about other ways that God speaks and how to activate yourself to start hearing in like manner.

Likewise, if you are just starting out in hearing the voice of God, make the decision upfront that you are going to go all of the way. We are now going to move on and talk about an important anointing that you need to help you hear the voice of God.

-3-

The "Detective Anointing"

A Burning Question

"Excuse me, Pastor Hector," the girl said looking quite nervous as she bit her bottom lip. "Do you have a quick minute? I just want to ask you a question."

It was a Saturday afternoon, and I had just completed a class on learning how to develop the gift of prophecy. I was tired and, quite frankly, just wanted to get out of the seminar and go home to relax and enjoy the rest of the day. I knew, however, that it was customary for many of the students to want to talk to the teacher after the class. I realized that it was part of the territory, so I got used to making myself available afterward for questions.

"Sure! I have a minute to answer your question," I replied.

"Well, I have a burning question. I believe that we have a mutual friend — Amanda (not her real name)."

"Oh, yes. Amanda is one of my leaders." At the time I was overseeing the prophetic ministry at the church I attended. Amanda was one of the youngest members of the ministry who showed so much promise in the prophetic. She truly had a strong gifting and I continued to feel compelled to mentor her in her gifting. I had known by observation that Amanda was truly sensitive to the voice of God.

"Okay, well, Amanda always says things that puzzle me," she blurted.

"Really? What kind of things does she say?"

"Well, let me give you an example," the nervous girl said as she let out a sigh and swept a curl of hair with her hand and tucked it behind her left ear. "Every time we go places she'll always find something that "confirms" her prayers. One time we were out, and we saw a billboard sign, and after Amanda read it, she said, 'Wow, God used the sign to confirm to me something He had been speaking to me'. Now, my question is this." The nervous girl exhaled as if trying to gather courage for her ensuing question. "God doesn't do stuff like that, right?"

"God doesn't do stuff like what?" I responded, pressing for a more concrete question.

"God doesn't always speak to us through everything we see, right? I find it flaky when people are looking at every door knob to see if God is speaking to them." With that, the nervous girl finally brought forth her issue. Even as she spoke the words, there was a judgmental look that came across her face. It was as if she was begging me to confirm to her that Amanda was a flake.

"Yes, God does speak to us in many different ways and one of those ways is by speaking to us through our surroundings," I answered firmly. "Amanda has disciplined herself to watch for God in everything. I would suggest that you ask God to help you do the same. You'll be amazed how much God sends things our way on a daily basis that we don't perceive."

"Really?" The girl was shocked. With the way she was looking at me, I soon realized that in her eyes I had become the flake! I almost felt bad that I was dropping this on her, but I knew that she had to learn how to come up higher in hearing God's voice.

"For the people who train their eyes and ears," I continued, "God will speak to them supernaturally on a daily basis. It requires that one develop discernment to discern the voice of God around them. I can enter a place with someone else and we could both be looking at the same scenario before us. It amazes me how I could perceive the voice of God through an event that takes place before me and yet the person next to me might be unaware the God was even speaking. It takes training."

"Wow, I never looked at it that way," she confessed. "Thanks for your time."

As she walked away, I wondered if she really accepted my words to her. I prayed that she would decide to walk deeper with God in knowing His voice. I couldn't help but wonder how many of God's children are in that exact frame of mind.

The "Detective Anointing"

God wants a body of believers who are trained up to hear from Him. It is time that we move from having a "hit or miss" experience to a place where we have a constant flow of "proven" communication from God in our lives. In order for us to get there, we must receive a "detective anointing".

You may be wondering, what exactly is the "detective anointing"? This is a phrase that I have coined…so allow me to explain. A detective is an investigator that is hired to solve a mystery surrounding a crime. There are many unsolved mysteries that require the expertise of detectives.

Detectives usually come from the ranks of the police force, however, one does not need police experience to be a detective. Some detectives are private investigators. These are people who have the proper licensing to function as a "detective for hire". That's where the term "Private I's" or "Private Eyes" comes from.

When detectives open a case, they compile all of the facts with the purpose of solving the case. Detectives will conduct investigations by interviewing people, studying the crime scene and by looking at all of the information from all angles. What is the detective looking for? Clues! Clues that will help them crack the case.

Detectives ask themselves questions such as: *What is the motive of the individual committing the crime? Why did it take place at that location? Who would be capable of such a thing?* They probe, investigate, search, research and then probe some more. They get into the mind frame of the criminal to try to understand the way the criminal thought.

Also, with today's technological breakthroughs, detectives are able to crack unsolved mysteries from many years ago. Old closed cases are being reopened because of the success detectives are having with the new forensic capabilities.

Another important aspect about detectives is their tenacity – they don't give up easily! If they gave up easily every time a case was difficult, the majority of crimes would go unsolved! On the contrary, detectives are very intense and tenacious in their pursuit to solve a crime. Detectives are specially trained in how to continue to dig for clues even after months of digging.

Similar to the job of a detective, the "detective anointing" is an anointing received from the Holy Spirit to search out God's communication. Why do we need a "detective anointing" to hear from God? God will many times conceal His communication from us so that we could uncover it. Proverbs 25:2 says, "*It is the glory of God to conceal a matter, but the glory of kings is to search out a matter.*" These "gems" of revelation that God conceals from us will be uncovered *only* by the trained eye that is looking for them.

If Jesus Christ is your personal Savior, then God has provided His communication for you as part of the salvation package. Just as we enjoy salvation, we should also enjoy His constant guidance and communication from the Father. It is His intention that we enjoy a constant flow of communication from heaven.

Detectives cover a large span of fields. Some detectives are involved in solving crimes involving fraud. Others are involved in crimes against children. Now we have detectives that solve technological or computer crimes due to the information age we live in. We have a calling from God to be detectives to solve the puzzle of what God is saying to us. We are to discern the voice of God in our every day lives. In order to be successful at hearing His voice daily, we have to do our part to discern His voice that He's concealed around us. It takes a trained detective to see God's "fingerprint" on things we encounter in our day that God has put there to talk to us.

A Cartoon

When I was first learning this concept of searching out the voice of God in my daily life, God used a cartoon one day to confirm the concept to me. My two daughters loved to watch a certain cartoon every day. We had just rented a video of that cartoon from the library so I wasn't surprised at the request for the video. I placed the disc in the DVD player and sat down in the living room with the purpose of journaling a dream that I had the night before.

As I was sitting in the living room writing in my journal, the cartoon my daughters were watching started catching my attention. Finally, I looked up from my writing to see what it was about.

In this cartoon, a young man had a pet dog. The young man would ask the dog questions that had to be figured out. On this specific episode, the young man asked the dog what it wanted to drink. Suddenly the dog indicated that it would answer the question by playing a game. So, as they played this game, the dog ran through the house and put a paw print on three items. As the young man walked around the house, he looked for paw prints. He found all three paw prints: one on a glass cup, the second on an ice cube and the last one on a lemon. After finding each paw print, he would write the clue into his notebook. When all three clues were found, the young man sat down in his thinking chair and brainstormed all three clues to solve the mystery. He finally put all the clues together and realized the dog wanted to drink lemonade. His success at figuring what the dog wanted to drink culminated in a huge song and dance that the young man and his dog enjoyed together.

I was shocked! I couldn't believe that God had confirmed to me through a cartoon what He had been showing me in every day life – His method of communication! Just like the cartoon, as a response to our prayers, God goes ahead of us in our day and places "God-clues" in our day for us to hear His voice. As we're going through our day, we are to look for these "God-clues", which are things that God uses to talk to us. We are to do a detective's work and find those clues and put those in our journal. As we gather enough clues, we must sit down and meditate and solve the mystery of what God is saying to us. The more we get used to doing this, the quicker we become at solving the mysteries surrounding concealed revelation.

We need this anointing because we need to start seeing deeper – beyond the surface. Oh, I can imagine how frustrated God gets with us as He puts many clues in our way to speak to us and we don't even notice His communication. Even if you think that you are not a good candidate for hearing God on a daily basis, you are. You don't have to be analytical or have previous police experience. This "detective anointing" is an anointing of the Holy Spirit and He will give it to those who are hungry enough to ask. Remember, God wants you to hear His voice, so of course He will help you. Let's look at reasons why you would want this anointing.

The detective anointing is necessary because:

1 – God speaks through many ways.

2 – God speaks in various volumes.

1 – God Speaks through Many Ways

Throughout history God has been very creative in the way in which He communicated with His people. We read in the Bible how God spoke through angels, with His voice, through a burning bush, through a donkey, through prophets, through orchestrated events, etc.. Hebrews 1:1 says, "*God, who at various times and in various ways spoke in time past to the fathers by the prophets…*" God is a not only a communicator, but He is a God who will use many different ways to communicate.

The question I get asked by many people is, "*Why does God do that? Is it to further confuse us?*" Of course my answer is a strong "*No.*" God is not the author of confusion.

To answer the question of why God speaks in so many different ways, let me first make this statement: God is a smart God. God knows how to do things that will bring forth maximum benefit for all parties involved. Remember, God is after the same thing that you and I are after — an intimate relationship. Therefore, in His wisdom, He created many different ways to speak to us that would not only bring us closer to Him, but would cause us to rely on His continual input.

God speaks in many different ways simply so that we could have confirmations! He set it up that way so that we could not only hear from Him, but so that we could *be sure* that we've heard from Him.

We need confirmations! They are so essential to hearing the

voice of God. Without them we will continue to walk in confusion and uncertainty. There are many reasons why we need to be confident that we are receiving a sure word from the Lord.

Confirmations are helpful because there are many different voices in the world today. All day long we are bombarded with voices that come at us from different angles sharing their various perspectives. We have family and friends who are quick to share their opinions with us. We have the media that constantly releases its biased views on what is going on in the world. We have the demonic realm that is always trying to hinder the work of God. We have our own thoughts and intellect that will battle against everything that God says to us. These are just a few examples of voices that constantly try to drown out what we receive from God.

Our detective anointing will help us investigate and filter through the junk. We don't want revelation from counterfeit voices! We want only the voice of the Shepard – only His voice will we follow! Therefore, God will speak the same thing to us through different methods so that we will know that we are hearing His voice accurately.

2 – God's Volume Button

Another reason for needing the "detective anointing" is because God doesn't always speak loudly. Our main preference, as believers, is to hear from God when He speaks in profound, dramatic ways. Therefore, we are all awaiting the direct prophetic word from the prophet or for the Archangel Gabriel to make his entrance into our mundane world to proclaim God's message to us. While it *can* happen that way, it's rare that God speaks loudly to us on an ongoing basis. The sad result is that there are many Christians who are busy looking for God's loud communication and are missing out on all of the subtle things that God is speaking.

As a proud father of two beautiful girls, I am committed to fostering a relationship of open communication to train them up in the fear of the Lord. Basically, what that means is that just as I spend time with them playing and having fun, there are times when I have to sit down with them to correct something that was done wrong.

Regularly, I adjust the volume and tone of my voice to fit the moment of communication. During corrective conversations I make sure to use my soft, loving voice so that my daughters know that while I am correcting them, I am doing it out of my love for them. With that same principle, when I need to be firm on a matter I use a more authoritative tone. Even though I will use the louder voice if I have to, I don't want to have to speak loudly to my daughters all the time. I want them to obey me even when I speak softly to them.

Can you imagine what it would be like having to use a strong authoritative voice every time you wanted your kids, employees, or anyone under your authority to obey you? If I used *only* a constant military tone to correct my daughters and require their obedience, they might get used to it and not take me seriously if I spoke with a tender tone. As a result, they would be used to responding only to loud communication.

In the body of Christ, there are many of us that have done exactly that – we have trained ourselves to only respond to God's loud communication. In order to shift out from that way of thinking, we must understand that God has a volume button.

God uses various volumes to communicate with us. When He speaks loudly, the revelation that we receive from Him is vivid because He is emphasizing a point. When He speaks softly, the revelation is faint – but nonetheless He is speaking. I've heard believers say things such as, "I know that I had a dream from God because the dream was so vivid." That kind of statement is usually given by people who are ignorant of God's various levels of volume.

Let's look some more into the life of Elijah the Prophet. After he scored that tremendous victory on Mt. Carmel, the Bible says in 1 Kings 19 that Queen Jezebel threatened to kill him, causing the prophet to run for his life. This same prophet that was successful in having God respond from heaven with fire is now fleeing for his life.

After walking a day's journey into the wilderness, Elijah sat under a broom tree and asked God to take his life. The response from heaven – an angel from God woke him up twice to feed him for the journey that was before him – a loud method of communication, if you ask me. Elijah then continued the 40 day journey in the wilderness until he reached Mt. Horeb – the mount of God. God had ordained a meeting to speak to His servant.

> *There he went into a cave and spent the night. And the word of the LORD came to him, "What are you doing here, Elijah?" He replied, "I have been very zealous for the LORD God Almighty. The Israelites have rejected your covenant, broken down your altars, and put your prophets to death with the sword. I am the only one left, and now they are trying to kill me too." The LORD said, "Go out and stand on the mountain in the presence of the LORD, for the LORD is about to pass by."* **Then a great and powerful wind** *tore the mountains apart and shattered the rocks before the LORD,* **but the LORD was not in the wind.** *After the* **wind there was an earthquake, but the LORD was not in the earthquake.** *After the earthquake* **came a fire, but the LORD was not in the fire.** *And after the fire* **came a gentle whisper.** **When Elijah heard it,** *he pulled his cloak over his face and went out and stood at the mouth of the cave.* **Then a voice said to him, "What are you doing here, Elijah?"** *1 Kings 19:9-13 (emphasis mine)*

God told Elijah to go out on the mountain because He was going to be passing by. So Elijah did exactly that. Now as Elijah waited for God to pass by, he heard a powerful wind – loud volume. Then, there was an earthquake – loud volume. Then there was a fire – more loud volume. However, even though the previous events were loud, the Bible says that **God wasn't in any of them**.

Elijah knew God's voice! After all, he served as a prophet of the Lord. Prophets are mouthpieces for God. Before they can speak for God, they have to hear what God is saying. So a prophet's complete ministry is wrapped up in their ability to hear from God accurately and their ability to communicate that message. Throughout Elijah's ministry in Israel, he was established as a prophet who was accurate and operated in the power of God – he knew God's voice.

After witnessing those loud events on the mountain, however, Elijah was not moved. He knew by experience that even though the events were strong enough to get his attention that it was void of God's presence. If Elijah would have miscalculated, he could have chased the earthquake, or the fire or the strong winds and would have missed how God chose to speak to him.

We read that after the loud events came a gentle whisper. That was it – an unromantic, undramatic gentle whisper. For some believers, soft communication would not be enough for them; they would be disappointed. Elijah, on the other hand, discerned God's presence in that whisper and "when he heard it, pulled his cloak over his face and went out and stood at the mouth of the cave". He knew that God was in that whisper and covered himself and went out to meet God. The fact that he covered himself confirms to us that Elijah was ready to meet God because he knew that God told Moses, "You cannot see My face, for no one may see Me and live." (Exodus 34:20)

This is the very area where many of us get tripped up. We have heard testimonies of dramatic ways that God spoke to someone else, and we expect the same for ourselves, and anything less leads to disappointment with God. Somehow we have been trained to believe that we could dictate to God which method and with what volume He is to communicate to us.

There are times when God uses the loud events to talk to us. He may be emphasizing a point or may want you to know His answer without a shadow of a doubt. Regularly, however, God uses soft to medium volumes to communicate with us regarding our daily lives.

At the church where I attend, I have taught a class on Hearing the Voice of God for many years. What I share with my students is to retrain themselves regarding God's volume levels. Rather than expecting only loud communication, I challenge them to train them-selves up to hear God's softer communication. By default, if you can hear the softer communication, you are definitely going to pick up the loud events that God sends your way. You don't need much training to hear from God in the loud events – it's the soft ones that require training to perceive.

Two Blind Men

Let's look at an example from Scripture how we can miss God's communication when our senses are not sharpened to discern God in our daily events.

After Jesus was offered up as a sacrifice on the cross, the Bible says that he resurrected after three days. After His resurrection, there were several things that He did. One of the items on His agenda was to take a trip to Emmaus. Let's look at that portion of Scripture.

"Now behold, two of them were traveling that same day to a village called Emmaus, which was seven miles from Jerusalem. And they talked together of all these things which had happened. **So it was, while they conversed and reasoned, that Jesus Himself drew near and went with them. But their eyes were restrained, so that they did not know Him**. And He said to them, "What kind of conversation *is* this that you have with one another as you walk and are sad?" Then the one whose name was Cleopas answered and said to Him, "Are You the only stranger in Jerusalem, and have You not known the things which happened there in these days?" And He said to them, "What things?" So they said to Him, "The things concerning Jesus of Nazareth, who was a Prophet mighty in deed and word before God and all the people, and how the chief priests and our rulers delivered Him to be condemned to death, and crucified Him. But we were hoping that it was He who was going to redeem Israel. Indeed, besides all this, today is the third day since these things happened. Yes, and certain women of our company, who arrived at the tomb early, astonished us. When they did not find His body, they came saying that they had also seen a vision of angels who said He was alive. And certain of those *who were* with us went to the tomb and found *it* just as the women had said; but Him they did not see." **Then He said to them, "O foolish ones, and slow of heart to believe in all that the prophets have spoken!** Ought not the Christ to have suffered these things and to enter into His glory?" And beginning at Moses and all the Prophets, He expounded to them in all the Scriptures the things concerning Himself. Then they drew near to the village where they were going, and He indicated that He would have gone farther. But they constrained Him, saying, "Abide with us, for it is toward evening, and the day is far spent." And He went in to stay with them. Now it came to pass, as He sat at the table with them, that He took bread, blessed and broke *it,* and gave it to them. **Then their eyes were opened and they knew Him; and He vanished from their sight. And they said to one another, "Did not our heart burn within us while He talked with us on the road, and while He opened the Scriptures to us?"** So they rose up that very hour and returned to Jerusalem, and found the eleven and those *who were* with them gathered together, saying, "The Lord is risen indeed, and has appeared to Simon!" And they told about the things *that had happened* on the road, and how He was known to them in the breaking of bread." Luke 24:13-35 (emphasis mine)

Can you believe it? While these two guys were able to see in the natural realm, they were blinded to what was going on in the spiritual realm. They had the very Jesus that they were talking about walking right next to them, and they didn't even know it. They had no clue who they were talking to until their eyes were opened. It took them all that walk to Emmaus and having a meal before they realized that Jesus was their companion. We need to be aware of God so that we don't miss hearing His voice.

Many times as we go through our day, we're not exactly aware of all that God has placed around us to talk to us. We must learn to develop a seeing eye, a hearing ear and a discerning heart to be able to detect when God Himself is speaking to us. I know by experience that the more that we do this, the easier it becomes with time.

Detective Skills

Okay, so now that you agree that you could do better in discerning God's voice, and now that I have your attention and your willingness to move forward to accept the "Detective Anointing", let's take the next step. There are skills that detectives utilize that we'll have to train ourselves in. These skills will help us learn to discern God's voice on a daily basis.

Be Alert – Don't go through your day oblivious to the fact that God wants to speak to you. Be alert! Know that your goal is to hear His voice on a daily basis. Assure yourself that He is speaking to you and that you are looking to catch any and all communication that He sends your way. A detective does not walk through a crime scene nonchalantly — they are alert to every detail.

We need to be God-conscience — aware of Him at all times and aware that He may use any method at any time to talk to us. Being alert and observant is something that you could easily train yourself to do with practice.

Connect the Dots – Detectives can look at a crime scene and connect the dots between when the crime occurred, how the criminal got away, and potential places where the criminal could now be hiding. All of the clues that the detective collects are to create a timeline of events in order to build a solid case that will result in the capture and arrest of the main suspect(s). We need to learn how to do the same.

In our busy lives, we will usually pray to God and ask that He moves on our behalf in certain areas of our lives. Then, we walk away from that prayer and completely forget that we asked for God's intervention. God, Faithful as He is, will then respond to our prayer by sending His angels. The angels will do God's will by orchestrating events for God to speak to us through, but being that we are so forgetful, we walk right through those events without a clue that we are receiving the answer to our prayer. From the moment that you pray to God for an answer, *look for God to respond.* Then connect the response to the prayers that you've been praying. Do the work of a detective: pray, be alert, get the clues, tie them back to your prayer and give God glory.

One night I woke up from a deep sleep and I heard myself saying, "Lord, I want to see my angel." Not knowing where those words were coming from, I dismissed them as words from an unfinished dream. Rather than trying to get back to sleep, I decided to go downstairs and pray for sometime. During my prayer time, I suddenly knew that there was a man in my house. I wasn't fearful, but I knew that I was not alone. Suddenly, in my living room, I saw the silhouette of a man. He was bronze colored, with short dark hair and was wrapped in auburn, gold, blue and yellow colors. He looked powerful! I was stunned when I saw him and in my ignorance I asked, "Is that Jesus?" Suddenly the Holy Spirit responded in my spirit and said to me, "You asked to see your angel." I was shocked that the request I heard myself say was valid. From then on, whenever I would operate in my gift of prophecy I would see blue streaks and would have a "knowing" (revelation in my spirit) that this angel was very active in my ministry. If the Holy Spirit hadn't reminded me of the strange request that I heard bursting from my mouth, I wouldn't have connected the dots as to why I was seeing this angel.

Document, document, document! – Your ability to stay on top of what God is sending your way is closely tied to your ability to keep a steady count of what you've heard. I can almost hear the moans and the groans already. Here's where the objections start to come in. "Do you mean to tell me that I have to keep a running account of

God's communications? How would I do that if my life is busy already?"

Well, bottom line, this part separates the curious from the hungry. Our flesh does not want to pay the price to grow spiritually. We want everything to come to us without any exerted strength from our part. However, if we are looking to increase our hearing God's voice, the old adage "no pain, no gain" fits. We must be willing to carve out time to document what God is saying to us. There is just no way around this point and there are no shortcuts. Here are some documentation options:

Journal – Keep a written journal of all of the communication that God sends your way. More journal tips in a later chapter.

Tape Recorder – You could record your voice speaking the received revelation onto a cassette or digital recorder. I do have to give a warning for those choosing this method. I have tried this method and after I filled a whole cassette with daily pieces of revelation that God sent my way, it broke. Two months of daily revelation were destroyed when I couldn't fix the cassette. Treat cassettes very delicately.

Any other method – Get creative. If you're not one to journal or don't have a tape recorder, get creative. The important thing is that you find some way to capture God's voice when He speaks to you. We live in the technological age that makes available to us new and more effective gadgets with recording capability. Have the Lord guide you in which device would suite your lifestyle best.

Receive the "detective anointing" from God. Practice the detective skills that we just covered and get ready to hear God speak to you. Now, the next chapter deals with a very crucial part of our success as "Anointed Detectives."

-4-
Let's Use Discernment

*"But solid food belongs to those who are of full age, that is, **those who by reason of use have exercised their senses to discern both good and evil.**" Hebrews 5:14 (emphasis mine)*

Another word for discernment is to "distinguish". All believers have a measure of discernment to know which voice is communicating with us. Now, you may have noticed that some of us have more than others. The reason for this, according to the above Scripture, is that discernment has to be developed by reason of use. We have to be users of our discernment. So, let's go over how to do this in an exact manner.

There are Many Voices

I have taught the class "Hearing the Voice of God" for many years in my church. As a custom, on the first day of every semester, I would start off by going around the room and asking people to share what they wanted to learn from the class. The majority would always say that they wanted to be sure it was God's voice that they were hearing because they didn't want to be led astray. Not surprisingly, this same response would be voiced over and over. I soon realized that many believers are hearing voices – they are just not sure whose voice it is. This is why discernment is so paramount.

Unfortunately, we hear various reports on the news of people who killed someone only to say that God told them to do it. We are alerted of people who commit heinous crimes in the name of "God". These events occur quite regularly and always leave a very sour taste in society's mouth. Currently, anyone today that says that they can hear the voice of God will be labeled as crazy.

The good news is that we know that you don't have to be crazy to hear the voice of God. Thankfully, we serve a God who enjoys communicating with His children and continues to do so today. Society in general does not understand this due to their lack of

understanding God. However, we believers must do our due dili-
gence to ensure that as we hear from God, we are staying safe from
other voices.

There are some strong reasons why we always need to be
certain that it's God's voice we are listening to and following. In the
previous chapter, I already introduced the concept that there are
many other voices in the world today. I also mentioned that God's
voice is at times a faint voice and that He may speak through many
different ways.   All of these are very important reasons as to why we
need to make sure that we are listening to the right voice.

The Counterfeit Bag

A few years ago, my wife came home with a gift that a friend had
given her. It was a very nice designer bag. At the time, I didn't know
much about designer bags or about that kind of industry.

After my wife asked for my opinion about the bag, I confessed
that I didn't know much about that stuff, but added that I thought it
looked nice. She then said to me, "No, what I mean is could you tell
that it's a knock-off?" I was shocked at the question and asked,
"What do you mean it's a knock-off? Why would you have a knock-
off bag?"

"Well," she replied, "my friend bought it for me as a gift. You
know the original bags from this specific designer are very expensive
and my friend couldn't afford it. So instead, she bought me a knock-
off just so that I'd know she had good intentions." My wife loving her
friend very much, took it all in good stride. I, however, was uncomfortable knowing that my wife would be walking around with such a
bag.

My wife clarified with me that normally she wouldn't carry around
such a bag, but just so that her friend would know that she appreciated the thought of the gift, she would use it. So after that discussion, I saw my wife using the counterfeit bag on a few occasions.
Now that I was made aware of that designer, I began to notice a large
group of women carrying the same kind of bag and couldn't help
wondering if they were counterfeits or originals. I decided to take
action and talk to someone who knew much about the fashion

industry – my secretary Tina.

Tina and her husband Bernard, youth pastors in their local church, were very good friends of ours. Tina, however, had another ministry — she was a phenomenal fashion consultant. She was very faithful to tell my wife and I when I had to shred certain ties that I wore, or what colors were "in" for that season. My wife and I highly esteem her fashion advice. (Truth be told, Tina has to be credited for the many beautiful gifts that my wife received. Again, her shopping guidance has been invaluable.)

I approached Tina and asked for her opinion about the knock-off bag. I knew what she was going to say wasn't good news because Tina shrieked in horror when I mentioned the knock-off bag. She said, "Well, the fact that your wife is using it is just a sign that she is a good friend." With that, Tina confirmed what I already knew – this wasn't a good thing.

Ironically, during that season, I saw a segment on an investigative show about the knock-off industry. These shops lock into a designer's fashion line and begin to produce counterfeits of all of their work. Because they use inferior materials, they are able to market identical bags as the original designers, for a fraction of the cost. According to this show, I learned that it is easier and less expensive to just let these shops continue to operate. Even after shutting down one of these shops, three to four others spring up in its place. It's a very lucrative market for these shops and they are very easy to set up and hard to squelch. That answered my question as to why they didn't close these places down.

After seeing that show, I started complaining aloud to God about these shops. The fact that they were making profit on a designer's design really was a hard thing for me to accept.

One day while I was in prayer about something completely different, the Lord spoke ever so softly to me, "Buy Barbie an original designer bag." "Why do You want me to do that?" I asked several times, but just continued to hear God repeat the same command. With Tina's guidance, I found the website for the designer. When I saw the prices on the original bags I wondered if they confused the price with the item number. They were expensive! I spoke to myself that I was a child of the King and that God would provide and ordered a bag for my wife. You should have seen the look on her face when she opened the parcel.

My wife now proudly uses her original bag. I feel proud knowing that she has the real thing because, after all, she's worth it. This experience, however, taught me about what designers suffer at the hand of counterfeiters who are looking to profit from their creations.

Satan the Master Counterfeiter

In the same way, Satan thrives on counterfeiting off of God's original designs! He is not creative in and of himself – he cannot create. All he can do is counterfeit what God has created and try to imitate it.

God created us so that we could have intimacy with Him. He desired to have a relationship with His creation. Part of that relationship involved our continual communicating with Him.

Satan, on the other hand, has another goal – our demise. Just as his fate is sealed to an eternal doom, he is looking to take as many of God's children down with him. He knows that if he could interrupt our relationship with God, that we would end up sharing in his doom. Nothing would make Satan happier except than to steal us away from God so that we could share in his death sentence for all eternity.

I can imagine that when Satan saw God speaking with His creation in the Garden of Eden that he was filled with awe. After all, God didn't continually commune with the animals or any other creature. It was different, though, with man and woman. God spoke to them and spent time with them. After spying and seeing how God expressed His love by communicating, I imagine that Satan had a brilliant idea – to talk to man and woman with the purpose of turning them away from God. He then entered the serpent and deceived Adam and Eve. That event marked the beginning of the counterfeiting industry!

Since that moment in time, Satan has set up his "knock-off shops" to mimic communication from God. There are many influences in the world today that are knock-off products inspired from

God's originals. The Bible warns us about Satan's counterfeiting schemes.

> *But what I do, I will also continue to do, that I may cut off the opportunity from those who desire an opportunity to be regarded just as we are in the things of which they boast. For such are false apostles, deceitful workers, transforming themselves into apostles of Christ. And no wonder!* **For Satan himself transforms himself into an angel of light.** *Therefore it is no great thing if his ministers also transform themselves into ministers of righteousness, whose end will be according to their works. 2 Corinthians 11:12-15 (emphasis mine)*

This Scripture highlights the fact that Satan will transform himself to deceive. Why would he have to transform himself into an angel of light? He would have to do that because there is no light in him. He counterfeits what God does.

Three Heavens

There are three heavens. Heaven one is the heaven that we see when we look up at our sky and the realm of outer space. Heaven two is an intersecting dimension that weaves through and around our world, from which Satan launches his attacks. Heaven three is where God's throne is established and where He rules from on high and yet it also weaves through and around our world. His throne is above all thrones!

> **Indeed heaven and the highest heavens belong to the LORD your God,** *also the earth with all that is in it. Deuteronomy 10:14 (emphasis mine)*

The Apostle Paul was caught up there and was given revelations from God.

> *"It is doubtless not profitable for me to boast. I will come to visions and revelations of the Lord: I know a man in Christ who fourteen years ago—whether in the body I do not know, or whether out of the body I do not know, God knows—***such a one was caught up to the third heaven.** *And I know such a man—whether in the body or out of the body I do not know, God knows—* **how he was caught up into Paradise and heard inexpressible words, which**

it is not lawful for a man to utter." 2 Corinthians 12:1-4 (emphasis mine)

Paul was caught up into the third heaven, where God is, and was given powerful revelations. The third heaven is where God's throne is and revelations from that realm are inspired by Him.

Satan the counterfeiter also has a realm from which he works and operates – heavenly places.

> *"For we do not wrestle against flesh and blood, but against principalities, against powers, against the rulers of the darkness of this age, against spiritual hosts of wickedness **in the heavenly places**." Ephesians 6:12 (emphasis mine)*

This point is not to be confused – although Satan operates from heavenly places, it doesn't mean that he is in God's heaven. Remember that Satan was cast out of heaven.

> *"And war broke out in heaven: Michael and his angels fought with the dragon; and the dragon and his angels fought, **but they did not prevail, nor was a place found for them in heaven any longer. So the great dragon was cast out, that serpent of old, called the Devil and Satan, who deceives the whole world; he was cast to the earth, and his angels were cast out with him." Revelation 12:7-9 (emphasis mine)*

Satan and his cohorts were kicked out of the third heaven and now their goal is to deceive the world. There is an unseen world wrapped around our world that is working very hard to keep us from accepting God's plan for our lives. Satan, the leader of this unseen world, plots and executes strategies to lead us further astray from God.

> *"But even if our gospel is veiled, it is veiled to those who are perishing, whose minds the god of this age has blinded, who do not believe, lest the light of the gospel of the glory of Christ, who is the image of God, should shine on them." 2 Corinthians 4:3-4*

This news shouldn't worry us. After all, our God has His throne established above all others. Even with all that Satan plots and plans, our God looks down over them and is aware and acts to prevent Satan from being successful. We have a promise that for those who fear God, God will protect. We can rest on that and live in peace. We shouldn't be at all fearful of the devil but have a strong confidence that God watches over us. We should, however, be aware of the enemy's schemes and conduct ourselves with wisdom to avoid falling into one of his snares.

> *"...lest Satan should take advantage of us; for we are not ignorant of his devices."* 2 Corinthians 2:11

While God does protect us, Satan can take advantage of us if we are ignorant of his devices. What devices? That he will use anything to stop you from following God. He knows that in order to follow God you must allow yourself to be led by God. Therefore, he will try to mimic God's communication in an attempt to confuse you or to lead you astray. The enemy can only be successful with this tactic if you are not aware of God's original communication and Satan's counterfeit communication.

Let me ask you a question. Is there such a thing as a counterfeit three-dollar bill? I'm sure you are responding that there isn't, and you would be right. The reason why there is no counterfeit three-dollar bill is because there is no original three-dollar bill. The counterfeiter who makes one up and goes to a store to try to spend it will immediately get arrested! A counterfeiter would never counterfeit something that doesn't have an original draft.

In order to understand how Satan attempts to counterfeit God's communication, we need to first learn the ways that God communicates. In the following chapters, I will go into details regarding the various methods God uses to speak and how to start hearing Him more in those methods. There are ways to know, however, who the communicator is behind a voice.

A Contrast Between Communications

Let's look at a contrast between God-inspired communication and communication that is from Satan to deceive and confuse.

1 – Peace versus Fear

Whenever God speaks to you, He will always give you an answer of peace. Even if He is giving you a warning or correction for a mistake, God will always speak it to you as an answer of peace. When God warned Pharaoh through a dream that Egypt would have 7 years of severe famine, Joseph conveyed that message to Pharaoh as an "answer of peace." (Genesis 41:16) Pharaoh was able to make plans to prevent the Egyptians from perishing in the famine thanks to God's answer of peace.

Satan's communication, on the other hand, is always injected with fear. He wants to infuse you with fear because fear cripples us from moving forward and holds us prisoners. Fear is not just an emotion, it's a demonic spirit that looks to have inroads into people's lives to destroy them.

> *"For God has not given us a **spirit of fear**, but of power and of love and of a sound mind." 2 Timothy 1:7 (emphasis mine)*

You can usually identify Satan as the communicator when the message is infused with a spirit of fear. If Satan can get us to open the door to that spirit of fear, he will have the opportunity to put us in spiritual bondage. At that point, the only way to be free of that spirit would be the power of Jesus Christ. We would need deliverance to command that spirit to leave us and to stop oppressing us.

Now I've heard people say that God has spoken to them things that left them afraid. Allow me to highlight the difference. It says in Proverbs that the "fear of the Lord is the beginning of wisdom." God will always prod us to fear the Lord so that we won't sin against Him. However, God does not want us to be afraid of Him and not approach Him as a loving Father. He is not the author of fear and will never want you living your life afraid of Him. Remember, God wants a relationship with you.

2 – Led to God versus Led away from God

God wants you to be led by Him. While He does speak in many ways, when you gather all of it together, it will lead you in the same direction – towards Him. Jesus said in John 10 that, "His sheep hear His voice and follow Him and the voice of a stranger they will not follow." God will always lead you to closer to Him, not away from Him.

Satan communicates to lead people away from God. One of his successful strategies in leading people away from God is to bring confusion. He will have many voices whispering different things to you all at once so that you find yourself lost in a whirlwind of communication. You thought you heard, "Go right," but then when you started to the right you heard, "Go left." It has you going back and forth and you start getting dizzy and not sure which way to go. That is a good sign that Satan is trying to deceive you with confusion.

> *"But God is not the author of confusion, but of peace…"*
> *1 Corinthians 14:33*

We have all gone through moments in our lives where were not sure which way to go. Confusion on this level is usually due to our lack of knowing God's true voice. This type of confusion usually diminishes once a believer activates his ability to hear the voice of God in all of the ways God speaks.

If after a believer is activated in hearing God's voice and confusion begins to come against them, that would be a clear sign of the enemy looking to distort. The solution is to take authority over confusing spirits and command them to leave. This usually clears the air so that we could press on hearing from heaven.

3 – Relationship versus Religion

Our heavenly Father will lead you deeper into an intimate relationship with Him. He wants you to be free to enjoy Him. Satan, on the other hand, will lead you into religious works. He doesn't mind if you're religious, as long as you are not growing in intimacy with God. The devil knows that it is possible to serve God and not know Him. Therefore, he will try to get you to focus on rules and traditions rather the liberty that Christ came to bring.

4 – Fruit of the Spirit versus Works of the Flesh

The result of hearing the voice of God is seeing fruit in the life of the believer. There is clear spiritual growth within the person. Developing the character of Christ and the fruit of the Spirit becomes evident.

> *"But the fruit of the Spirit is love, joy, peace, longsuffering, kindness, goodness, faithfulness, gentleness, self-control..."*
> *Galatians 5:22-23*

I have been asked by some about the overall purpose of the gifts of the Holy Spirit. My response to that question is a resounding, "To bear much fruit!" It's that simple. God wants us fine-tuned in hearing His voice so that we could bear much fruit and be effective in what we're called to do.

Not so with the devil! Anything that he reveals or speaks will be with the purpose of promoting unrighteousness. Another way to look at this is that if you find yourself acting out the works of the flesh as a result of revelation, it could be a sure sign that the communicator was Satan. Let's define what the works of the flesh are:

> *"Now the works of the flesh are evident, which are: adultery, fornication, uncleanness, lewdness, idolatry, sorcery, hatred, contentions, jealousies, outbursts of wrath, selfish ambitions, dissensions, heresies, envy, murders, drunkenness, revelries, and the like; of which I tell you beforehand, just as I also told you in time past, that those who practice such things will not inherit the kingdom of God."* *Galatians 5:19-21*

Now let's use our common sense. Why would God give us revelation that would stir up the works of the flesh knowing that these could prevent us from inheriting His kingdom? He wouldn't! All that God reveals draws us into His righteousness.

So when you receive revelation, ask yourself what is the fruit of that revelation. How does the revelation expect you to respond? By looking at the fruit of the revelation, we unmask the communicator. This is a great discernment tool. Let's look at a few examples.

> *Example 1:* Let's say that you run into a long-term friend that you haven't seen in a while. You and this friend have left things off on a bad note. Something in the friendship went awry and things were never repaired. As you see your friend, you get a sudden prompt in your spirit to forgive. You approach your friend and apologize for not making things right sooner, but you do your part to reconnect with them.

Who could this revelation have come from? It's obvious that God was the communicator behind the prompting. Why? One of the components of the fruit of the Spirit is love. Others are peace, kindness and goodness. This revelation has God's stamp on it. This fruit of the Spirit is the character of Jesus. As we are led by God to grow the fruit, we begin to become transformed into the image of Jesus.

> *Example 2:* You are at work and you're having a bad day. Suddenly as you look at a coworker, you see her saying something about you to another coworker and the two of them begin to laugh. You know that you are the reason for their laughter. Suddenly, an almost audible voice speaks to you and tells you to wait for them after work in the parking lot and give them the "whooping" of their life. Your thoughts chime in and tell you that such a "whooping" would teach them not to mess with you.

Who could be behind this revelation? This one is just as obvious – the communicator would be Satan. Why? One of the works of the flesh is outbursts of wrath. God would not want you to beat anyone up to teach him a lesson. That type of revelation would be a huge clue that Satan is flooding your inbox with junk mail.

Discernment Checklist

For this reason, God gave me the idea of using a discernment checklist. As a good detective, your job (should you choose to accept it) is to make sure that you sift through pieces of revelation that come your way. What is the goal? The goal is to keep only the revelation that comes from God. Anything else you need to immediately discard. Okay, let's go over our checklist:

1 – Does it contradict Scripture?

If any revelation that you receive contradicts Scripture, throw it out! That means that when a voice tells you to divorce your faithful wife and marry another woman because she's more spiritual or attractive, take that revelation and burn it! Why? Because according to Scriptures you would be entering into an adulterous affair. God will never lead you into an adulterous affair. Never! All revelations must be supported with Scripture and must never contradict any of it. Other examples of false revelation that would be in direct violation of Scripture are:

~ Murder - God would never ask you to kill anyone.

~ Lies – God detests lies and would never promote it.

~ Theft – Don't blame stealing on God. If you read the Scriptures, you'll see that He does not tolerate this sin either.

~ Sexual Immorality – If you read in the book of Revelation, you may be surprised to read that a lot of those who could not enter His kingdom, couldn't enter due to their sexual perversions.

There are many more examples that I could give, but unfortunately, that would be a book in itself. Therefore, I'll leave you with this exhortation: know the Scriptures and know what God accepts and abhors. Knowing the Scriptures will be a major discerning tool to help you sift through the voices that speak to you. God will never speak against His written word.

2 – Does it give you peace?

Remember, God always gives an answer of peace. Now, don't misunderstand me. God has a way of challenging, stretching and molding us that may make us afraid. We should be firm, however, about knowing that it's all out of love for us. He may even reveal something futuristic/apocalyptic to us and even then it's not right to fear. We must trust His protection over us and His love for us. If after receiving revelation you are tormented by fear, it should be thrown away as something erroneous.

3 – Can you share it with anyone?

God wants us to grow responsibly. For that reason, the Bible says that, "…in the multitude of counselors there is safety." (Proverbs 11:14) That doesn't mean that we tell everybody what God showed us, but we can wisely share it with Godly people that we trust to help guide us. Satan, on the other hand, tries to get us separate from the pack to attack us. After all, that is how predators work. Predators will attack a herd and try to cause a lot of confusion by running circles around the pack and create a stampede. Once they get the majority of the pack running, they go for the smaller, weaker ones that fall behind or that somehow get separated from the herd. Spiritually, Satan does the exact same thing. He will always try to get us to be "lone rangers" and not to be accountable to anyone else. Therefore, any revelation that requires that you keep it secret and not share with your spouse or pastor you should question immediately. Your spiritual life may depend on your ability to do so.

4 – Does it confirm what God has been speaking to you?

Many times, God will talk to us repeatedly about something and then will speak for the last time as a confirmation. Well, if God has been telling me through many ways that He wants me to teach the Scriptures and then I get a prophetic word about teaching, that would be a confirming word. It is a good sign when God repeats something to us – it confirms to us that we're hearing accurately. Now, remember that the other side to this coin is that God always starts talking to you about something at some point. So just because it's the first time that you've heard about a topic from God doesn't mean you can't accept it. Just begin to look to see if He starts speaking to you in other ways to confirm it. If you believe that God is speaking to you about something and confirmations never come, then I would say put it to the side and don't do anything with it unless God speaks further to you. A detective can never solve a case just by uncovering one clue. They solve the case by piecing the clues together to get insurmountable evidence. We must do the same to be sure that we are hearing accurately.

5 – Does it fit with God's character?

Remember, God is a holy God. He is wise, powerful, loving, nurturing, faithful, etc. If you receive revelation that God hates your guts, it would not fit God's character. Therefore, that revelation must be thrown out. Some people may have a problem with this point because they don't know God's character. They must come to know His character by reading the Scriptures. Once, in my Hearing God's Voice class, when I reached this point, a woman raised her hand and said, "Yeah, but God told Abraham to kill his son. That didn't fit God's character, and yet God spoke it." I then explained that while God did speak it to Abraham, it was never about Isaac being killed. It was about Abraham being obedient and trusting in God's provision. God had to test the "father of many nations" by seeing if he would give up his only son. There was a purpose in the magnitude of this trial. It was also a prophetic picture of what God was getting ready to do – offer His only Son. God had a purpose in testing Abraham that way, and only Abraham. He never tested any other person in the same way. Bottom line – use this rule of thumb: If it doesn't fit God's character…it isn't Him.

So, I would say, use this checklist any time you receive revelation to judge it. As you grow, you'll find yourself using it less because you're activating discernment in your spirit. Just as Hebrews 5:14 promises, "by reason of use we develop our spiritual senses to discern between both good and evil". Protect yourself from other voices and use your discernment.

- 5 -
Hindrances

A Friend in Need

"Hector, you don't understand. I can't hear anything at all. I try to get God to talk to me and He doesn't. What's the problem? What am I doing wrong?"

My friend was down and out. He was frustrated at the lack of hearing God's voice. There were some important decisions that he needed to make and could not hear God's words to him. He sat there across from me at the coffee shop feeling defeated and disappointed.

On the exterior, he was dressed for success. His cashmere trench coat was crisp and sharp; it looked new. Underneath he wore a bright-white starched shirt. He sported a stylish hairstyle. His hands were manicured and smooth. The stylish aura around my friend matched his handsome look and his air of professionalism. Not one thing about him would be the picture of defeat, and yet here he was at the very precipice of despair. I was awed at the contrast.

"You're not doing anything wrong," I chided. "You have asked God to speak to you, and now you have to be alert to hear from Him. You have to believe that you can hear the voice of God. If you approach God doubting His desire and ability to talk with you, then you're making it harder to hear. You need child-like faith to believe. Just believe."

"How do you believe?" he asked.

"You believe by repenting for unbelief and ask God to help you believe. You also believe by getting into the Scriptures and reading God's thoughts towards you. Such as when Jesus said in the book of John that His sheep hear His voice and are led by Him."

"Well, what if that doesn't work?" he rebutted.

"It will work if you believe. God is not a liar. Believe Him! He wants to talk to you more than you want to hear from Him."

With that, a look came across my friend's face that sealed the conversation. I knew what it meant – he didn't believe me. He thanked me for my time and went on his way. I was sad for him because I knew that the problem was his unbelief.

A Hearing Problem

With that encounter, I realized that many people have spiritual hearing problems. They can't hear the voice of God regularly. They know that God speaks today, but for one reason or another, they cannot hear continually. They have a "hit or miss" experience. That is not God's will for their lives.

If we are not hearing regularly from God, we are missing out on a lot. God wants to talk to you about every area of your life. He is a practical God and is concerned with all of the details of your life. In order to have an increase of God's communication, let's first correct any hearing problems.

Let's look at what some hindrances are to hearing God's voice.

Negative Faith

As in my friend's case, a lot of people cannot hear the voice of God because they are exercising negative faith. Negative faith is putting our faith in other things rather than in God.

Every believer has a measure of faith.

> "...as God has dealt to each one a measure of faith." Romans 12:3

With the measure that is dealt to us, we must do our part to make it grow. Many of us pray, "God, increase my faith." God then responds to us, "No, *you* increase your faith." According to the word of God, we know that we increase our faith by:

~ Hearing the word (Romans 10:17)

~ Praying in the Holy Ghost (Jude 1:20)

~ Meditating on and confessing the Scriptures (Joshua 1:8)

Increasing our faith is our choice. We could leave it just as it is. Rather than believing God's promises, it is much easier to use that faith and put it in something else other than God. Faith is a tool that was given to us for our use. Whether you know it or not, you are putting your faith in *something.* That something that you're believing in is bringing forward your current results. When we put our faith in something other than God, this is what I call negative faith.

~ By not believing for God's healing, you are putting your faith in your ability to stay sick.

~ By not believing for God's provision and prosperity, you are using your faith to believe for poverty.

~By not believing for God to provide you a spouse, you are using your faith to believe that you will stay single forever.

~By not believing that God loves you and wants to bless you, you are using your faith to believe in the lie that you're not as good as everyone else and that God is out to keep you unsuccessful.

On the same token, by not believing that God wants to communicate with you and that you can hear the voice of God, you are using your faith to believe that you cannot hear from God and that He doesn't want to talk to you.

Faith is a powerful tool that will work whether we know it or not. If we don't purposefully release it to believe in God's promises, we will use it to believe and produce the very things we fear and the insecurities that we struggle against.

You may think that the reason you cannot have breakthrough is because you have a lack of faith. That's not entirely true. You have faith – it's just that you've misplaced it. You've placed it in something other than God. If you're not getting your breakthrough, it probably means that it's time for you to place your faith back in God's promises.

If you find yourself doubting that you could hear God's voice, you are going to have to take action to renew your mind. You can do this by getting your heart settled on the promises from God's word. Begin to speak Bible promises over yourself until you believe them. Insert your name into the Scriptures and say them aloud. To build my faith to hear from God, I always declare the verse from John 10 over myself, "Hector is Jesus' sheep, and Hector can hear His voice. God knows Hector, and Hector follows Him."

Practice this until you have your faith built up to hear from God. By being willing to take your misplaced faith and put it back into believing God, you'll start seeing a huge difference. Remember that it takes faith to please and engage God. As you start developing that faith, God will take notice and will reward you for seeking Him.

The Nazareth spirit

> *"Now it came to pass, when Jesus had finished these parables, that He departed from there. When He had come to His own country, He taught them in their synagogue, so that they were astonished and said, **"Where did this Man get this wisdom and these mighty works? Is this not the carpenter's son? Is not His mother called Mary? And His brothers James, Joses, Simon, and Judas? And His sisters, are they not all with us? Where then did this Man get all these things?" So they were offended at Him.** But Jesus said to them, "A prophet is not without honor except in his own country and in his own house." **Now He did not do many mighty works there because of their unbelief.**"* Matthew 13:53-58 *(emphasis mine)*

I find it amazing that Jesus was rejected in Nazareth. Even though they knew Him, they never credited Him for His tremendous character. They were offended by Him only because He was from their village. They were biased against Him because He was from Nazareth. How sad when we miss God's blessings because we can't receive the vessel God uses.

These people were familiar with Jesus because they saw Him grow up in their town. They knew that Jesus' family lived a simple, humble life, and they judged Him by it. They couldn't receive His great anointing because, in their eyes, He was no one special.

Therefore, the "Nazareth spirit" is that spirit of familiarity that discounts the voice of God because of the details. Some may have this type of spirit, and they can't hear God speaking to them at church because the pastor may be a relative. People with this spirit also won't receive a prophetic word from anyone at their church due to the fact that they know the messenger.

This type of familiarity is a hindrance. You could tell the type of individuals who have this spirit because they are always asking God to use people who do not know them or their situation. That type of bartering with God is wrong. It's not our place to tell God how to speak to us. Rather, we should be alert to discern His voice through whatever means He uses.

God has spoken to me many times through my wife, my mother and even my children. Oh, how I praise God when He can even use those close to me to communicate a message to my life. I would miss out on God's words for me if I said, "Now, God, that's only my wife talking. She knows me and only wants to give me her opinion. So, use someone from another church to call me and tell me the same message." If God moves my wife as a mouthpiece, I will listen. If God moves my pastor with counsel for me, I will listen. We must listen and discern.

Shake off the Nazareth spirit of familiarity off of you. Allow God to use even those around you to be messengers to you. Remember, whether God uses a friend or a stranger as a mouthpiece – it's all still God speaking to us.

Lack of Teaching / Wrong Teaching

Some cannot hear from God because they were never taught how to. Others grew up in denominations or in settings that denied God's communication for today. Either way, the concept that God talks today is a new one for them.

I am of a particular school of thought that the things of the Spirit could be taught. I've heard far too many people say that when it comes to hearing from God, you either have it or you don't. Not so! With sound Biblical teaching, we can help even those with spiritual hearing problems begin to flow in a stream of communication from God.

Today we need New Testament prophets to take their place more than ever. According to Ephesians 4, prophets are those who equip the believers for the work of the ministry. What do they equip in? They equip believers on how to hear the voice of God and how to develop their spiritual gifts. While those in the office of teacher can do an effective job, the prophet will not only teach and equip, but will also go beyond the teacher by imparting an anointing to hear God's voice. This comes from their ministry mantle to hear the secrets of God and to be mouthpieces for the Lord. Any five-fold minister can instruct on hearing the voice of God, but it goes so much deeper when the teaching can come from a seasoned prophet.

Sin

Sin is something that keeps us apart from God. God, in His continual invitation to us to come closer to Him, has established that we must aim to live free from sin. Now, while none of us are without sin, there is a huge difference between a sinful nature and a continual lifestyle of sin. Therefore, believers who live in continual sin will find themselves lacking in their communication from God.

> ***"For if we sin willfully after we have received the knowledge of the truth, there no longer remains a sacrifice for sins,*** *but a certain fearful expectation of judgment, and fiery indignation which will devour the adversaries. Anyone who has rejected Moses' law dies without mercy on the testimony of two or three witnesses.* ***Of how much worse punishment, do you suppose, will he be thought worthy who has trampled the Son of God underfoot, counted the blood of the covenant by which he was sanctified a common thing, and insulted the Spirit of grace?*** *For we know Him who said, "Vengeance is Mine, I will repay," says the Lord. And again, "The LORD will judge His people." It is a fearful thing to fall into the hands of the living God." Hebrews 10:26-31 (emphasis mine)*

The opposite of living a sinful life is to live a life of holiness. The good news is that God has already provided everything that you need to live a godly life – including holiness.

> *"Grace and peace be multiplied to you in the knowledge of God and of Jesus our Lord,* ***as His divine power has given to us all things***

that pertain to life and godliness, through the knowledge of Him who called us by glory and virtue, by which have been given to us exceedingly great and precious promises, that through these you may be partakers of the divine nature, having escaped the corruption that is in the world through lust." *2 Peter 1:2-4 (emphasis mine)*

Our focus should be on walking in the Spirit, and by default, we don't fulfill the lusts of the flesh. Some of us really need to catch this revelation. Many believers spend their days trying to talk themselves out of sinning. If this is you, your focus is in the wrong place. Stop your fruitless striving and begin to accept what God has already made available to you. We are holy because He has provided holiness for us. Put your focus on walking in the Spirit. By walking in the Spirit, the lusts of the flesh lose their strength in us. Every time we revert back to the flesh, those desires come back alive. The only way to live in victory over the works of the flesh is to stay in the Spirit, and by doing so, you keep your flesh crucified on the cross. Walking in the Spirit will cause communication from His throne to flow.

Fear

You've probably heard by now the acronym for fear.

F.E.A.R. = False Evidence Appearing Real

Fear is not from God. In chapter three we already dealt with the issue of the spirit of fear. Fear is a demonic spirit that wants to entrap us in demonic phobias to keep us from trusting in a protective Father. Here are some basic fears that will hinder our hearing from God:

Fear of being deceived — Some people, no matter how much you try to set their minds at ease, are overly concerned of being deceived. It's so strong that it's a fear. Or, better put, the spirit of fear has them in bondage in this area. If we belong to God, we must trust in His protection. We already talked about how to use our discernment to identify anything that comes from Satan so that we can throw it out. By knowing the Scriptures, using our discernment and having a multitude of counselors, we can walk securely knowing that God will protect us from the devil. If we're looking to hear the voice of God more, let's find comfort in the following verses:

"Or what man is there among you who, if his son asks for bread, will give him a stone? Or if he asks for a fish, will he give him a serpent? If you then, being evil, know how to give good gifts to your children, how much more will your Father who is in heaven give good things to those who ask Him!" Matthew 7:9-11

Fear of rejection – We have all, at some level, feared being rejected. However, God will not reject you! The Scriptures promise, *"Draw near to God, and He will draw near to you."* (James 4:8) If you would but only be so daring as to take the first steps towards cultivating a hearing ear, God would take the same steps toward you. Go for it! You will not regret it.

Fear of God – Occasionally, I've encountered believers who are afraid of what God would say to them. They have an image of a fire breathing God who is looking to burn them to a crisp. Their perception of God is like the mythological god Zeus who is vengeful and is waiting for a chance to throw a lightning bolt right at us. Or they may be living in sin and are convinced that God wants to kill them. Either way, this type of fear exposes a lack of knowing God's character. While He is in fact an awesome, fearful God, He is loving and yearns for us. This type of fear can be overcome by getting a revelation of who God is.

Fear of the future – Our God holds the future in His hands. Some are afraid of knowing what lies ahead. They are afraid that hearing the voice of God would mean that God would begin to tell us the scary things that they'll have to endure. Not so! You see, God knows what you and I could handle. What would it benefit God to speak to us only to further push us into fear? Let's use our common sense. God will talk to us about our future out of His desire to bless us and to show us what He has in store for us. That is not to be feared but to be enjoyed. It's a perk of being a child of God.

There are many more fears that may hinder us from hearing the voice of God. The bottom line is that if you struggle with fear, you can be set free. God never gave you that spirit, and He doesn't want you to keep it. Ask your spiritual leaders to pray with you for deliverance so that you could be free from this spirit of bondage and so that you could enter into your place of liberty.

Out of Alignment

We are a triune being! We are a spirit, we have a soul and we live in a body. Oh, what a beautiful creation we are!

Spirit – With our spirits, we commune with God. Here is where Jesus dwells in us when we accept Him as Lord and Savior. The kingdom of God dwells within our spirits. This is what is meant when we say that we are born again. Before Christ, our spirits were dead in our sins. When we accept Christ, our spirit man comes alive with the life of God. It is our spirits that thirst after intimacy with God.

Soul – Our soul houses three components: mind, will and emotions. With our souls we are in touch with our own thoughts, desires, and feelings, which serves to form our personalities. God created us with a soul so that we wouldn't be robotic. Each person has their own unique makeup that makes us funny, serious, dramatic, clever, etc. God created our souls so that we could have spiritual thoughts, a submissive will and godly emotions. However, our soul, in its carnal sinful nature, rebels against God. It must be transformed through prayers of submission and through renewing our minds in the Scriptures.

Body — This is the shell that we live in. With our bodies we are in touch with the world around us. Without a body, we would not be able to live in this world. This body that was taken from the dust, goes back to the dust when we die. It is the spirit man that lives eternally.

God created man perfectly and placed him in the Garden of Eden. Man was created in perfect alignment with his three components. God created man's spirit to rule over the rest of his being since his spirit would be submitted to God's will. Man's soul was submitted to his spirit, and his body was submitted to his soul. This was a picture of perfect alignment.

However, we know that Satan tempted Adam and Eve to sin against God. As a result, man's perfect alignment was shattered when he placed his own will above God's. Remember, the will is in the soul realm and, therefore, man placed his soul above his spirit. Now the soul of man was sitting on the throne in man's life. That was not God's design, and it cost man dearly to be unaligned. We can see, as we read through the Bible, the consequences of that sin. Man chose to walk selfishly instead of being led by God.

Jesus came to set the record straight. Not only did He die on the cross, He also submitted the exalted soul to the spirit of man. You see, when Jesus prayed in Gethsemane, He asked God to spare Him from the cross.

> "Then Jesus came with them to a place called Gethsemane, and said to the disciples, 'Sit here while I go and pray over there.' And He took with Him Peter and the two sons of Zebedee, and He began to be sorrowful and deeply distressed. Then He said to them, '**My soul is exceedingly sorrowful, even to death**. Stay here and watch with Me.' He went a little farther and fell on His face, and prayed, saying, '**O My Father, if it is possible, let this cup pass from Me; nevertheless, not as I will, but as You will**.'" Matthew 26:36-39 (emphasis mine)

Why do you think Jesus' soul was sorrowful even unto death? The soul didn't want to lose its place of authority! The soul of man knew that it was about to be given a death-blow and sent back to its original place – submission to the spirit. Jesus prayed that God would spare Him the cross but concluded, "nevertheless, not as I will, but as You will." Well, we know that it was God's will for Him to be offered up as a sacrifice, and therefore, Jesus laid down the desires of His soul and submitted Himself to God's will. With that, Jesus not only reconciled us with the Father, He also forced the soul back to submission.

As a result, we can now walk in perfect alignment. We can once again enjoy the fruit of having our spirit man dictate to the rest of our being how we are going to walk. We don't have to be led by our souls anymore. You don't have to be living life according to your emotions or your traumas. You can turn that in and live a life led by the Holy Spirit through your spirit. We must get in right alignment with God.

I've come to the realization that some people can't hear accurately from God because they still have their souls sitting on the thrones of their lives. They have their minds, wills and emotions exalted above God's will for their lives. Then they wonder why God doesn't talk to them as He does to others. You have to get *yourself* out of the way. You are out of alignment! Your soul, unless it's submitted to your spirit, will always fight and oppose the things of God. Your exalted soul together with your body creates what the Bible calls "the flesh". This "flesh" is at war with your spirit man and does not want to submit. However, if you want to live a life full of God's blessings and communication, you must get into proper alignment.

How do you get into alignment? You can do so by easily praying a prayer of repentance. Ask God to forgive you for exalting your soul above Him. Then, speak over yourself. Tell your spirit man to come alive and to submit to the leading of the Holy Spirit. Tell your soul and body to submit to the leading of the Holy Spirit. By praying this prayer of alignment on a daily basis, you're reminding yourself that you choose a life of being led by the Spirit who abides in your spirit.

Positioning Yourself to Hear from God

Now that we've identified some basic hindrances to hearing God's voice, let's deal with these hindrances so that we can position ourselves to hear from God. The good news is that God doesn't only talk to those who are free. In His love, He will even communicate to those in bondage. However, He will never want us to stay in bondage.

Pray your prayer of deliverance. Come to God and ask Him to expose anything in your life that hinders your relationship with Him. Be ready to write down anything that He shows you and ask Him how to deal with each item. Be obedient to do all that He shows you. If you have to ask someone for forgiveness, do it. If you have to go and confess a sin to someone, go and do it. By being obedient, we could be free from all bondages and enjoy the liberty that Christ came to give.

Now that we know God speaks to us, that He designed us for intimacy, that we need to receive the "detective anointing", that we have to use our discernment and now that we are positioned before Him, let's learn about the ways that God uses to communicate. Let's study the puzzle pieces.

Section 11:

Understanding the Puzzle Pieces

– 6 –
Scriptures
{*Puzzle Piece #1*}

> **"For the word of God is living** and powerful, and sharper than any two-edged sword, piercing even to the division of soul and spirit, and of joints and marrow, and is a discerner of the thoughts and intents of the heart." Hebrews 4:12 (emphasis mine)

Did you know that God's word is a living word? It is! As you have read from the above verse, God will use His Scriptures to pierce the division of soul and spirit, joints and marrow, and it discerns the thoughts of our heart. Wow!

God speaks to us through the Scriptures. This is also one of the most common ways that we can discern what we are hearing from God. In order to appreciate how God speaks today through the Scriptures, there are three Greek words that we must learn: graphe, logos and rhema.

Graphe

According to the Greek Dictionary of the New Testament, graphe (pronounced gra-fay) means "a document".

Many people around the world only read the Scriptures as "graphe", written material. It is not a "living word" to them, but rather something they read for its literary value.

Sure, the Scriptures contain rich reading material. From cover to cover, all 66 books contain much interesting information. One could really enjoy reading about the major and minor prophets and their role in Israel. One could get lost reading the rich history of the Israelites. The poetry within its pages is exceptional. Therefore, it is possible to read the Scriptures and miss the message that God is sending you regarding salvation in Him.

"All Scripture is given by inspiration of God, and is profitable for doctrine, for reproof, for correction, for instruction in righteousness, that the man of God may be complete, thoroughly equipped for every good work."   *2 Timothy 3:16-17*

"...knowing this first, that no prophecy of Scripture is of any private interpretation, never came by the will of men, for prophecy never came by the will of man, but holy men of God spoke as they were moved by the Holy Spirit." 2 Peter 1:20-21

Did you catch that? The Scriptures were written as holy men of God were moved by the Holy Spirit to write its contents. The Bible is more than just an informational reference book. It is alive with God's life and contains God's thoughts toward you and the world.

I remember when I was looking to graduate with my Bachelor's degree. In order to get college credit for life experience, I had submitted a practicum regarding my knowledge in the Old and New Testaments as well as how I used that knowledge in ministry. After my evaluating professor read my document, she called me and said, "Hector, you've done a good job writing your papers."

"Thank you." I responded excitedly at the prospect of receiving the college credits.

"You're missing one thing, however." She replied.

"What's that?"

"You're missing criticisms of the Bible. In order to get credit for your Old and New Testament surveys you'll need some Bible criticisms."

"Why in the world would I ever want to criticize the Bible?"

"Well, Hector, there are many reasons. For one, many scholars don't believe that the book of John is authentic. They doubt it because of the large gap of time between when Jesus died and when the book of John was written. Also, they doubt its authenticity because of its striking contrast with the other gospels. So, I want you to find 3 critical views and include them in your paper."

I found myself dumbfounded and shocked that someone would teach Old and New Testament Surveys in a college and not believe its authenticity! My eyes were opened to the reality that some people look at the Bible only as "graphe" – written text.

Unfortunately, I had to write that report including three critical views of the Bible. However, I refused to give the critics the last word and criticized the critics at the end of my paper. I was surprised when I was granted those credits.

Logos

The Greek dictionary of the New Testament defines logos as "reasoning". This is where the word "logic" comes from. Logos represents the "logic" behind what is written or what is said.

Not only should we read the Bible, we should know the logic behind what is written. Unless we grow in the "logos" of the Scriptures, it will remain only "graphe" to us. We grow in the logos when we allow the Holy Spirit to illuminate us and reveal to us what God wants to show us from each verse.

I remember when the logic of one of my favorite Scriptures came alive to me one day. I used to work at a gospel radio station and came across a little book of Bible verses. I picked it up and began to thumb through it. My eyes fell on Psalms 46:1, *"God is our refuge and strength, a very present help in trouble."* When I read that verse, the part "very present help" struck a chord within my spirit. Then I was illuminated as to the logic of this verse. I then understood that God is not only a help in times of trouble, He is *a very present help*. God is establishing His faithfulness when we are in times of trials. Little did I know how soon I would have to draw strength from that verse.

At that time, I was working the morning shift at the radio station. The radio station would go off-air at midnight and would not go back on until morning. My job was to get there at 5:00 am and to get the station on the air at 5:30 am sharp! I was being counted on to have everything up and running at the right time.

I awoke one morning to very frigid temperatures. I drove to the radio station as per my normal routine. Upon arriving, my heart melted within me when I realized that the front door had a sheet of ice over it. In the frigid cold temperatures, there was ice on the lock, which prevented me from opening the door. While I could get the key in, I could not turn the lock – it was frozen!

I began to get desperate because time was ticking and I had to get the radio station on the air. I tried breathing hot air onto the lock, and then I tried banging on the lock…nothing happened. After feeling defeated, the Scripture that the Holy Spirit recently illuminated to me rose up from my spirit. I said it aloud, *"God is a very present help in trouble."* I realized that God was present with me! So I acted on the logic of that verse. Being that He was a very present help, I thought it only made sense to ask for His help. I prayed, *"God, You know that my responsibility is to get the radio station on the air on time. If I don't, I could get in major trouble with the boss and possibly lose my job. I learned from Your word that You are my very present help in trouble. I am in trouble. God, please help me get into the radio station. I need the ice in the lock to be melted so that I could open the door. I thank You for Your help in Jesus' name. Amen."*

I put the key in the door one more time and with no extra effort, turned the key. The key turned right before my very eyes! The key that wouldn't turn for me for 25 minutes in the frigid cold now turned supernaturally. I let out a victory shout to God and went into the station and got everything going right on time! God saved my job because I was illuminated with the logic of that verse that told me that God is my very present help in trouble.

To grow in the "logos", one goes beyond just what is written on the page. It's not enough to read that, "The Lord is my Shepherd." We must learn the "logos" and understand the revelation behind the verse. That verse basically means that you will not lack anything you need because God watches over you just as a shepherd watches over his sheep.

To grow in the "logos", we must understand that the message of the Scriptures applies to us today. Although the books have been written long ago, they are still practical for us today.

Rhema

The Greek Dictionary of the New Testament defines "rhema" as an utterance. Another way I call it is "a spoken word."

It's important to know the "graphe" Scriptures. We must know about creation, Adam and Eve and what happened at the Garden of Eden. It's important to learn about how man failed God and how God promised a Redeemer in Genesis 3:15. It's easier for us to understand what's going on in the world today by reading about God's plan for the nation of Israel. It's important to know the Gospels and how Jesus Christ was the promised Redeemer back in Genesis. It's important to know that the Holy Spirit came on the day of Pentecost and His role in the world today. It's crucial to know about the new covenant that Jesus brought through His sacrifice on the cross. Even if we are new to the family of God and don't understand much of the Bible, it's of high importance to get into the habit of reading the Scriptures. By doing so you begin your quest in growing in God.

As you continue to read the "graphe" Scriptures, even if they don't make much sense to you, the Holy Spirit can begin to illuminate your mind. That's when you begin to grow in the "logos" of the word. The more we read, the more God has to illuminate us so that we will not just read what's on the page, but how it applies to us today.

There is another level of communication, however, that many miss – rhema Scriptures. One major puzzle piece in hearing the voice of God is when He quickens a "rhema" Scripture to speak to us. There are times when we are reading Scriptures and suddenly a verse seems to jump off the page and speak to your very specific situation. If this has happened to you, you have experienced a rhema Scripture.

I opened this chapter by listing Hebrews 4:12 which says that, *"For the word of God is living and powerful…"* The Scriptures are not just a bunch of words thrown on a page. The Scriptures are the love letters from a living God to His children. He has a way of quickening certain Scriptures to our specific circumstances to speak to us. Only God can have the wisdom and the power to do such a thing.

God may even use a verse that you've read hundreds of times and you may even know by memory. However, as you're going through something in life, suddenly God may have the Scripture jump off the page and speak to your specific situation. He spoke to you through that verse. That is a "rhema" Scripture.

A "rhema" Scripture is different from that of a "logos". A "logos" Scripture is when you are illuminated to the meaning of a specific verse. You understood the logic behind it. A "rhema" Scripture is when God uses a verse to talk to you directly about a specific situation.

God speaks regularly to His children by quickening "rhema" Scriptures. It happens to some more than others because some have activated themselves to receive from Him in this way. Let me give you some modern day examples of how God does this.

Peace with the Beasts

My mother was called by God to serve as a missionary to the country of Mexico since I was a child. When I was only a baby, she was getting ready for bed one night when a booming, audible voice filled the room. It said, "You will go to Mexico for Me." Immediately, she knew the call was from God and that it would come to pass in His time.

My three siblings and I were very aware of my mother's call to Mexico. Throughout our teen years, we waited patiently knowing that the day would come when our mother would have to go. We all accepted her call but wondered how it would happen. God in His wisdom waited until I was to enter college as a freshman. Being the youngest of the four, and the one still living with her, I was the last one depending on her support. Everything had come together beautifully, and she knew that her timing was at hand. After dropping me off at my college, my mother said her goodbyes and left to launch her ministry in the country of Mexico.

It wasn't too long before the praise reports began filtering in as to how God was using my mother as an agent of change in the humble vicinity of Delicias, Chihuahua. She was instrumental in helping build a new church that was deteriorating. She did many home visits and led many to Christ. Most importantly, she assisted a pastor and his wife with their church duties giving them the much-needed assistance. It wasn't until years later, however, that I learned that my mother almost walked out on her call from God.

After returning home many years after serving in Mexico, I asked her if she ever had any desire to leave Mexico. She began to tell me about a major struggle that she had while down there.

She told me that living in that type of arid environment, there were many different kinds of animals that she was not used to. She had seen tarantulas, scorpions and all kinds of creatures and bugs that scared her. All throughout her stay, she would try to be strong and to take it all in stride – but one night that all changed.

As my mother was sleeping that night, something woke her up. The light in her room was flickering on and off. She wondered why her light be malfunctioning. As she lay in bed trying to make sense of it, she saw it. A scorpion was about to crawl onto her head. My mother jumped out of her bed, and with all the courage she could muster, killed the intruder.

My mother shared how she began to cry out of deep frustration. She began to pray and told God that either He would help her get over her deep fear of those kinds of animals, or that she would return home immediately. Suddenly, she felt compelled to go read her Bible. The Scripture below is the translation of the verse as it shows in the Spanish Bible. The translation reads like this:

> *"In that day, I will make a covenant **with you** and the beasts of the fields, and the birds of the air, and with the creeping things of the ground…to make **you** lie down safely." Hosea 2:18 (emphasis mine) (Reina Valera)*

God quickened a "rhema" Scripture that spoke to my mother's specific situation. When she read that verse, she was filled with much comfort knowing that God had spoken to her and that He was going to cause her to "lie down safely".

Look at how well that Scripture fit her circumstance. God in His Sovereignty knew that He would speak to her from that verse, and so

He led her to read it. It was more than a "logos" word, it was a Scripture that uttered God's very words to her situation. With that security, my mother was able to complete her ministry call in Mexico and supernaturally got over her fear of the creeping things of the ground.

An Annoying Co-Worker

I once worked for a community based organization in the center of the city of Rochester, New York. I really did enjoy my work there as a Program Manager and enjoyed taking a part of all of the outreach to the surrounding communities. I was experiencing favor with God and with man, and everything was going fine; well, almost everything. Even though I tried to stay positive while on the job, I began to realize that one of my co-workers was becoming a thorn in my side.

This co-worker, while she did a very professional job, made it clear that she did not like me. Every time we had a staff meeting, she would wait until I had ideas to then start bashing them in front of the rest of the staff. Her attacks on me were always deliberate. I tried being very nice to her, but no matter what I tried, she would continue that behavior. I also noticed that she would seem to turn other coworkers against me because some of them suddenly would stop talking to me. I witnessed quiet discussions in various rooms and somehow knew that I was the topic of the discussion. It was enough to make me dread going in to work every day.

After much thought, I concluded that the reason why this co-worker had an issue with me was because I held a higher ranked position within the company. I decided that I had only one option to address the problem – I was going to take this co-worker into the boss' office and confront her on her negative behavior. I wasn't looking to be her best friend, but I did want the two of us to work in the same office in peace.

The day came when I was going to go to my boss and request a meeting between the three of us. I had carefully planned how I would approach my boss and what words I would use. After praying that morning, I grabbed my keys getting ready to leave for work when a thought came to me, "*I haven't read the Scriptures this morning*". My usual habit was to pray and to read the Word before leaving for work. So, I found my Bible and sat down to read for a few minutes. I began reading in Matthew, when Joseph found out Mary was pregnant.

> *"Now the birth of Jesus Christ is as follows: After His mother Mary was betrothed to Joseph, before they came together, she was found with child of the Holy Spirit. Then Joseph her husband, being a just man, **and not wanting to make her a public example, was minded to put her away secretly**." Matthew 1:18-19 (emphasis mine)*

Suddenly, the words, *"and not wanting to make her a public example, was minded to put her away secretly,"* leapt off the page at me. With that verse, I knew that God had spoken His will to me in that situation. He didn't want me to take her to the boss to make a public example of her. He wanted me to deal with her in secret. I knew that I knew that I knew that God quickened that "rhema" Scripture to show me what He wanted me to do.

Now notice, the revelation was a "rhema" Scripture and not a "logos". Had it been a "logos", it would mean that the logic behind that verse would be that God wouldn't want us to make a public example of anyone at anytime. That's not true. There are times when God would lead us to deal with things publicly.

> *"Moreover if your brother sins against you, go and tell him his fault between you and him alone. If he hears you, you have gained your brother. **But if he will not hear, take with you one or two more, that 'by the mouth of two or three witnesses every word may be established'. And if he refuses to hear them, tell it to the church.** But if he refuses even to hear the church, let him be to you like a heathen and a tax collector." Matthew 18:15-17 (emphasis mine)*

God had not given me a "logos" illumination, but a "rhema" revelation. God was speaking in my specific case that He wanted me to handle this matter privately. How did I know that it was a "rhema" revelation of Scripture? Once I read it, it leaped off the page, and I felt that God spoke to me through it. Also, I felt a peace in my spirit that served as a confirmation that God was talking to me. My only way of explaining this phenomenon is to say that you'll know when it happens.

What happened with my co-worker? Well, I followed God's guidance. I went to work and asked her if she could give me 10 minutes of her time. We went into the conference room and with all of the wisdom that God was giving me, I spoke with her honestly sharing my concerns. I also made sure that everything about me showed her respect; the way that I sat, the way that I addressed her and the tone of my voice. We were able to clear up many misunderstandings and wrong perceptions. We shook hands and walked out of there agreeing to work well with each other. For the time that I remained at that agency, I can honestly tell you that this co-worker and I worked great together from that moment on.

Oh, how I praise God that He spoke to me and that I obeyed His word to me. I could have complained. I could have whined about how right I was to do what I was going to do. However, my goal has been to hear the voice of God and to obey Him. God gave me a chance to show Him that I meant business and that I was going to obey; even if I thought He was wrong. Maybe He led me that way to spare her the embarrassment. Maybe He knew things would get worse if I took her to my boss. I don't know why He told me to do it – I just listened, obeyed and enjoyed the great results.

God spoke to me in this specific case by quickening a Scripture to my specific situation. God will do that with you as well. If it has happened to you before, then you can relate. If it hasn't, activate your faith that God will speak to you the same way.

Activate Your Faith For "Rhema" Scriptures

We can't quicken Scriptures to ourselves anymore than we can make an angel come down from heaven to talk to us. That's the Holy Spirit's job. However, many times we don't hear from God a certain way because we are not aware of it and that it's available to us by faith. Now that you know that one of the ways to hear from God is by receiving "rhema" Scriptures, ask God to give you more. Sure, we can ask God to speak to us more in this way. Being that we know that it's God's will to speak to us, what do we have to do to see the increase of the communication?

Here's what I would advise you. Read your Bible daily. Have a reading program and stick to it. Some read their Bibles by following daily devotionals. Others read the Scriptures as they feel led that day. What's important is that you make sure that you read the Scriptures daily. While you are reading, if something seems to jump off the page and speak to you specifically, **consider** it as "rhema" revelation from God. Now that God has your attention, ask Him to confirm it through **another** way that He speaks, and He will be faithful to do so.

Remember, anything that you believe God is speaking to you **must** pass the discernment checklist. Also, remember not to run only on one piece of revelation that God gives you. He's expecting you to do your part as a responsible detective and find the confirmations you need before moving on what God showed you.

This is Just One Piece of the Puzzle

God speaks in many different ways to communicate and to confirm. The Scriptures say, *"By the mouth of two or three witnesses every word shall be established." (2 Corinthians 13:1)* If God gives you a rhema Scripture, ask Him to confirm it in another way that He speaks. Never act only on one Scripture that God gives. You must wait for confirmations. The Scriptures was only one of the witnesses. You need more to confirm His word. We get in trouble when we only act on one piece of revelation that God gives us. Rhema Scriptures go hand in hand with the other ways that God speaks. Let's look at another puzzle piece.

- 7 -
God-Thoughts
{Puzzle Piece #2}

"For My thoughts are not your thoughts, nor are your ways My ways." Isaiah 55:8

God has thoughts! He is constantly thinking about His children. What I think is cool is that not only does God have thoughts toward us, He wants to share them with us as well.

The Psalmist David expressed how much he valued God's thoughts.

"How precious also are Your thoughts to me, O God! How great is the sum of them." Psalms 139:17

David enjoyed knowing God's thoughts toward him – they gave him comfort and peace. We can know God's thoughts too! How, you ask? Well, the Scriptures say that we have the mind of Christ.

"For who has known the mind of the Lord so that he may instruct Him? ***But we have the mind of Christ****." 1 Corinthians 2:16 (emphasis mine)*

If we have the mind of Christ, then we can hear Christ's thoughts. Pretty simple.

This is one of the more regular ways that God speaks that we ignore. God will many times put His thoughts on our minds and rather than receive them, we usually think that we made them up and discard them.

Is it Me or God?

I get this question so many times from people who are not sure about these God-thoughts. "Is it me making it up?" they ask concerned. Many believe that they have been creating these thoughts in their own heads and take credit for them.

As a result of that thinking, we believe that we are the authors of all of our thoughts, both good and evil. We take credit for the thought that tells us that someone we know needs prayer or that we should give an offering to someone we know that's in need. On the other hand, we also condemn ourselves for the thought that tells us to take money out of a person's wallet that we discovered on the floor, or the thought to punch someone's face in when they are rude to us. Reality check – a thought that comes to your mind does not mean it originated from you!

If you can relate with the above mentioned examples, you are not aware of how evil and God-thoughts operate. They operate quite the same way in that they seem to be random. However, using our discernment checklist, we could easily sift between the two. God-thoughts, like any other form of revelation, must be tested by trial and error.

You would be amazed at how much God talks to you if you would only consider that God *may* be talking to you. Instead of taking credit for everything that floats through your thoughts, learn to discern them first. Yes, we do have our own thoughts. I'm constantly thinking about the outfit I want to buy, the bills I have to pay, the pizza that I want to eat for dinner. However, I am also aware of the evil thoughts that float through my mind and I know how to deal with them. I am also aware that God-thoughts will be a regular piece of communication that I have to be ready to identify and test through trial and error. Being aware that God will give you God-thoughts is half of the victory.

Evil Thoughts or God-Thoughts?

It's usually easier for us to identify evil thoughts as opposed to God-thoughts. We could be going about our usual day and suddenly have a terrible thought. We may suddenly get a thought to kill someone, or to commit adultery, or to steal some money from the company safe. Usually (hopefully) we could immediately identify that these evil-thoughts are not from God and throw them out. Now, we're pretty good at identifying evil thoughts, but we're not as good to identify a God-thought. We tend to struggle with the idea that because it came into our thoughts that we made it up and that it cannot be of God. That way of thinking just shows us how little we know about the ways that God communicates. Let's look at some ways to identify God-thoughts.

Random Communication

One way to identify God-thoughts is that they seem to come from out of nowhere. They are random in nature. In other words, you did not have your thoughts focused on the topic of the God-thought. You were thinking about something completely different when the God-thought suddenly introduced a new topic.

A typical example is when you are thinking about one thing and suddenly you start thinking about an old friend you haven't seen in a while. The thought seemed to have come out of nowhere, but it came. To your surprise, you run into that friend that very day and mention to them that they were just in your thoughts. Coincidence? I doubt it. The more we get familiar with God's voice, the less we'll believe in coincidences and more in God's providences. God-thoughts are random.

Repetitive

Repetitions are another way to identify God-thoughts. Many times, the Holy Spirit will speak to you by giving you a God-thought. At first you may throw it out thinking that you made it up. After a while, however, you notice that the thought came back. With that repetition, I would say, "pay attention"! Ask yourself, "Could God be speaking to me through this?"

When you get a repetitive thought, God may be using repetition to get your attention. We wouldn't be good detectives if it took God 50 times to speak something to get our attention. The reason why we're Anointed Detectives is because we're searching out to hear from Him. So if we get a random thought that catches our attention and the thought keeps coming back, let's accept that God may be speaking to us. Let's pray about it and test it through trial and error.

Reflects God's Character

All God-thoughts (like any other method of His communication) will represent God's character and will bear fruit in your life. It will be sent from the throne of God to be a blessing to your life. It will not take away from you, but it will edify you or someone else. You won't have to use much discernment when a thought tells you to run an annoying person down with your car. By default, you will know that it doesn't reflect God's character. Throw it out as an evil thought!

Now what?

Once a God-thought has your attention, depending on what it is, test it through trial and error. This will help you confirm if what you heard is accurate or not.

For example, let's say that you keep getting a thought to call your friend and to encourage him. The only way you're going to know that you're hearing accurately is to call your friend and test what you've heard.

Now don't go calling them up saying, "Joe Schmoe, I have a word of the Lord for you." You don't know if you have a word or not. Rather, test it with much humility. Let them know the thought that came to you and ask them if it makes any sense. If it does, great! If it doesn't, great! Either way, you stepped out to test it to see if it was a God-thought. God-thoughts are usually confirmed when what was revealed in our thoughts actually is confirmed in the situation.

The Incredibly Active Mind

A word of caution – our minds are incredibly active. Our brains were designed by God so that we could sort and store an incredible amount of information. Our brains are a gift from God. Without them we would not be able to process information.

Our mind, however, is a part of our soul. This is what we call "our thought-life". Every person has a thought life, which basically is your mind thinking all day long. Our thought lives are very active. If it weren't that way, we wouldn't remember to pay the rent, pick up the kids from school, or bring the tithes to church. We need our thought lives to stay on top of everything going on.

As we're looking to hear from God, many times our busy minds will interfere. That is why all thoughts must be tested through trial and error to see if they were originally from God or from the devil, or from our busy minds.

I once lost my car keys and could not find them anywhere. I was so frustrated because I was running late! After looking all over the place, I decided that I would give God the opportunity to reveal to me where they were. "God, please help me find my keys! I prayed in desperation. I stayed quiet to hear what God would speak to me. Suddenly a thought came out of nowhere, "Go check under the sofa." I ran to where the sofa was and looked underneath it and beneath every cushion. I didn't find the keys.

I closed my eyes again to hear what God would say to me. Another thought came to me, "Go check in the bathroom." I ran to the bathroom and turned everything over desperate to find my keys. To no avail. My keys weren't there. After about four attempts, I quit trying to hear from God due to the inaccuracies. Thankfully, my wife was able to find the keys on her own.

Later in the day, feeling discouraged at the outcome of my "hearing", I prayed and asked God why I couldn't hear an accurate answer. It wasn't until I was deep in prayer that I heard, "Hector, you were not able to hear My voice because your mind was busy trying to figure things out. In an effort to be on time you had all these thoughts already going through your head. You will always know it's Me when after you have tested the thought, the results will be accurate. By not finding your keys, you knew by default that I was not the Author of that thought. My thoughts will at times interrupt your other thoughts – and even then, they must be tested for accuracy."

With that I learned an important lesson about the busy mind. God will allow us to hear His thoughts, but we must be very careful not to assume that every thought is from God. In order to test the thoughts we believe are from God, it is important to use trial and error.

"Teach a Class."

One afternoon, I was at home spending time in prayer. As I paced the living room floor praying, the thought came out of nowhere, *"Teach a class at church on Hearing the Voice of God."* I was shocked! That was the farthest thing from my mind. I never thought of teaching a class, much less on that topic. Even though I practiced hearing God's voice, I never considered teaching a class on it. I concluded that I was being distracted from my prayer, and I threw it out and kept praying.

A few minutes later the same thought returned. *"I want you to teach a class at church on Hearing the Voice of God."* I realized that it could have been a God-thought. So, I responded, "Okay, God. You have my attention. I heard what You said. I'm going to make a note and approach Pastor Don next week and see if this gets confirmed through the circumstances." At that time, Pastor Don was the associate pastor at my church who was overseeing Wednesday night Bible classes.

The following week, I ran into Pastor Don at church. I approached him and said, "Pastor Don, I have to talk with you. I was praying the other day and the thought came to me to teach a class on Hearing the Voice of God. As you know, I've not taught a class here before, but if you feel that it would be beneficial, I would like to make myself available to do it." He responded, "Hector, that's a great idea. We just had a teacher drop out of the fall semester, and we have room for one more class. I was just praying and asking God which class to put in that slot. Your timing was impeccable." With that, God confirmed to me what I already knew: I was to teach this class. I taught the class for many years, and it was a tremendous blessing, not only for others, but for myself as well.

A Double-Message from God

When I was a young man in the Lord, I traveled with a group of Christian teens to a service in Buffalo, New York. This service was designed to minister to the teen crowd and to encourage them to go deeper in God.

The preacher delivered a powerful message about placing our all on the altar of the Lord. It was a well-prepared and well-delivered anointed message. As the sermon was closing, the preacher invited all of the teens to respond to the message by going to the altar. Immediately, the altar was packed with bodies of hungry teens looking to go further with God. I was among the crowd of teens who responded.

As I stood within the mass of people, I had my eyes closed and was praying a prayer of submission to God. The Holy Spirit was moving powerfully in our midst, and I knew that it was a holy moment in God's presence. Suddenly, in the middle of my prayer at the altar, this thought came to me out of the blue, "When *she* lays her hands on you, *I* am going to speak to you." "*She?*" I wondered. "*Who is she?*" As I opened my eyes, I saw that one of the ladies from the Buffalo area who brought a van full of teens to the event was at the altar praying for everyone. I found that odd because she wasn't the speaker and yet she was praying for every teen there. When I noticed her, she was about two teens over from where I was standing. So I just closed my eyes again and waited.

Quickly, she made her way to where I was. She laid her hands on me and began to pray in tongues. I stayed especially attentive waiting to hear if she would say anything to me. Suddenly she said, "The Lord says to you that He is raising you up for a special ministry. He has a holy work for you to do in His kingdom. He has seen your heart and is pleased with you. Know that while you cannot see the full picture, God has much in store for you. Trust Him to walk you into what He has for you." With those words she moved on to the next teen. I, however, exploded in tears as those words filled my hungry spirit. I cannot begin to tell you the peace that I felt surging through my being as she prophesied those destiny words over me. Not only did God speak to me through this woman, but He had spoken to me directly through a God-thought to prepare me for the messenger He was sending to me.

Only One Piece of the Puzzle

I don't mean to sound like a broken record; however, remember that God-thoughts are only 1 piece of the puzzle. Never make major changes based on what comes only through a God-thought. Remember, God-thoughts must be tested through trial and error, and they must go hand-in-hand with all of the other ways that God speaks.

Now that you have received a God-thought, ask God to confirm it in *another* way that He speaks. Remember, we can take advantage of the many puzzle pieces so that we can be sure that God is truly speaking to us.

-8 -
Our Spirit
{Puzzle Piece #3}

"The spirit of a man is the lamp of the Lord, searching all the inner depths of his heart." Proverbs 20:27

What happens when you place a candle in a dark room? You get illumination! A candle will illuminate and bring light to a dark place. What has God placed in our lives to bring illumination to us? A lamp – our spirits! It's not that our spirits can illuminate by themselves, but they can only illuminate if they have the light of God – the Holy Spirit.

As previously discussed in Chapter 4, it is in our spirit where the Holy Spirit resides when we accept Christ. The Holy Spirit will then begin His ministry in us to sanctify us, remind us Jesus' words, guide and teach us. It is in our spirits where many times we get communication from God. In order to increase the flow of communication in our spirits, we need to learn to become spirit-conscience. In other words, we need to train ourselves to learn to develop a sensitivity to what is going on in our spirits and embrace that as a legitimate way that God will speak to us.

Let's look at Proverbs 20:27 in the King James Version:

*"The spirit of man is the candle of the Lord, searching all the inward parts of **his belly**." Proverbs 20:27 (emphasis mine)*

Isn't it interesting that man's spirit searches all of the inward parts of our bellies? Why our bellies? Because I believe that it is in our midsections where the human spirit is located — at the very core of our being. Let's look at why God would allow communication to take place there.

The Second Brain

Did you know that our midsection is considered to be our second brain? Why? It's considered so because our digestive systems and guts are lined with over one-million nerve cells.[1] Whether you know it or not, you have two brains.

Did you ever wonder why when you get nervous you feel "butter-flies" in your stomach? Were you ever fearful of talking to someone and as you run into them you feel your heart "drop" into the pit of your stomach? Our insides are lined with many nerve cells that allow us to "feel" what our brains are thinking. So with the first brain we process information, and with the second one we can "feel" or "sense" good or bad things that result from the information we process.

"Yeah, but..."

I know, I know, I know. I can hear your objections already! "Yeah, but what you're stating promotes emotionalism." For those of you struggling with this rebuttal, I can sympathize with you. I also suffered from a "Westerner's Mentality" once.

You see, in the Western world, we have this mentality that every-thing that occurs is by coincidence and chance, or as others call it – luck. As believers, we have been bombarded by messages even from within the church that tells us that we are flakes if we believe that God will speak regularly to us. With people's attitudes, words and even with sermons we hear preached, the message to us is clear: Don't look to have a supernatural experience. Walk with your feet on the ground like the rest of us.

We have also heard so many messages against our feelings. We hear things such as, "Don't be led by your emotions. Only be led by God." "If you are moved by your emotions, then you are living in the flesh." Now, I can understand that the real message behind the exhortations are valid — we cannot make our life decisions by our *soulish emotions.* However, we have swayed from one side of the extreme to the other. We have gone from, "don't be led by soulish emotions" to "don't pay attention to your feelings because that's the voice of the flesh and you'll be led astray." Nowadays, we are ex-horted that it's not just soulish emotions that have to be ignored, but it's also *any* emotion that you feel. Not so!

By swaying from one extreme to the other, we are ignoring a very important method that God uses to communicate to us. God has created our temples (bodies) with great wisdom and He placed many nerve cells in our being as a way to allow us to sense certain things that He is saying to us through sensations in our spirits. What we need to develop is a discernment to distinguish between soulish emotions and sensations and promptings in our spirits that were created by the Holy Ghost to talk to us. The more you ignore communication in your spirit, the more calloused you become to what takes place there. On the other hand, the more you practice a sensitivity to the voice of God in your spirit, the more you'll become sensitive and the more communication that will take place there.

Just as the Holy Spirit uses our brains to speak God-thoughts to us, He will also use our second brains (our spirit) to speak in our spirits. God uses these feelings and sensations that we feel on our insides to communicate a deeper message to us. Let's look at how communication takes place on this level.

Urim and the Thummim

When God led His people out of Egypt and gave them the blueprints for the tabernacle and the order of service, He didn't fail to leave out instructions to receive His guidance. They were given specific instructions regarding the priest's garments. One specific part of their garment had to do with their ability to hear God's voice.

> *"And you shall put in the breastplate of judgment the **Urim and the Thummim, and they shall be over Aaron's heart when he goes in before the LORD. So Aaron shall bear the judgment of the children of Israel over his heart before the LORD continually.**"*
> *Exodus 28:30 (emphasis mine)*

Urim means "light", and Thummim means "perfection". These two items were placed within the breastplate of judgment for the priest to carry. While the Bible doesn't say much about what the Urim and Thummim were exactly, there are various theories of how they functioned.

The Urim and Thummim were two stone-like items that were placed in a sack that was worn by the priest behind the breastplate. One theory says that one stone was white and another was an off-color and by pulling the stone out after inquiring of the Lord, the priest would know God's will. Another theory says that both stones were extracted and that the one that would light up communicated God's will. At this point, again, we're just speculating because the details were not revealed. What we do know is that the priest would understand God's will in a certain situation by inquiring of the Lord through the Urim and the Thummim.

Now Moses, as the prophet, was hearing from God face to face regarding the bigger picture. On smaller more individual cases, the priest had the responsibility to hear from God by inquiring of the Urim and the Thummim. While they didn't have the direct face-to-face communication that Prophet Moses had, the revelation that they received through the Urim and Thummim was nonetheless accurate. By it, God would let them know whether His answer was a "yes" or a "no". That method would also indicate a person's guilt or innocence regarding a judgment.

As we continue to read the Old Testament, we see many different cases when the priest had to inquire of the Lord through the Urim and the Thummim. Here is one account.

In the Book of Ezra, we read about when the captives were returning from captivity in Babylon back to their own cities in Israel. In an effort to make an account for everyone, these were all reporting in their own cities for a census, which was to reconnect families.

> *"And these were the ones who came up from Tel Melah, Tel Harsha, Cherub, Addan, and Immer; but they could not identify their father's house or their genealogy, whether they were of Israel: the sons of Delaiah, the sons of Tobiah, and the sons of Nekoda, six hundred and fifty-two; and of the sons of the priests: the sons of Habaiah, the sons of Koz, and the sons of Barzillai, who took a wife of the daughters of Barzillai the Gileadite, and was called by their name. **These sought their listing among those who were registered by genealogy, but they were not found; therefore they were excluded from the priesthood as defiled. And the governor said to them that they should not eat of the most holy things till a priest could consult with the Urim and Thummim.**" Ezra 2:59-63 (emphasis mine)*

Notice that some of the sons of the priests could not find their listings. As a result, they were excluded from the priesthood as defiled and were told by the governor that they should not eat of the food that the other priests were eating from until they *consulted with the Urim and Thummim.* Remember, this was their method of hearing the voice of God to confirm if the person was innocent or guilty. These sons of the priests would have to wait for God to reveal His will through the Urim and the Thummim regarding their ability to return to their priestly duties.

I find the location of the Urim and the Thummim interesting. It was located behind the breastplate over the heart. The high priest carried it all the time. I'm sure that as he walked with his garments, he could feel the Urim and the Thummim pressing against his heart reminding him that he had access to the voice of God.

Well, while we don't physically have a Urim and a Thummim today stuffed inside our shirts and turtlenecks, we do carry them in our spirits. In the same way that God illuminated His will with a "yes or a "no" or a "guilty" or "innocent", the Holy Spirit will prompt our spirits with similar revelation.

"Yes" and "No"

Like the Urim and Thummim, the Holy Spirit could allow you to sense a "yes" or a "no" in your spirit when you're seeking God's direction. When this takes place, while you don't hear thunder or see lightning, you know on the inside of you that God said "yes" or "no".

"Innocent" or "Guilty"

Again like the Urim and the Thummim, the Holy Spirit will at times flash an "innocent" or "guilty" sense in our spirits to let us know the truth in a situation. Parents, we are usually more developed in this area. Even with the most convincing words, there are times when something in our spirit is indicating to us that what is being said is not true. Remember, if you are a temple of the Holy Spirit, then He is within you and will communicate from where He dwells in your being.

> *"But solid food belongs to those who are of full age, that is, **those who by reason of use have their senses exercised to discern between both good and evil.**" Hebrews 5:14 (emphasis mine)*

Every believer has a level of discernment and the more we use it the more we develop it. How do we use and develop it? We do so by being sensitive to the senses that we have in our spirits.

Now, I'm not saying that all senses we feel in our spirits are God-inspired senses. Not at all. Again, we have to develop discernment to know when it is the Spirit of God and when it's not. The more we become sensitive and aware of what's going on in our spirits, the more we give God something to work with in us.

A word of caution: never use a sense that you have in your spirit to hurl accusations against anyone. Even when God does give us discernment in our spirits, He, being a wise God, will confirm it to us through other ways and will give us the wisdom on what to do with that revelation. God will show you what to do with what He reveals to you. All you have to do is to be aware that He is speaking to you.

Inner Witness

> *"The Spirit Himself bears witness with our spirit* that we are children of God." *Romans 8:16 (emphasis mine)*

Another word for witness is "assurance". Sometimes the Holy Spirit will give us a witness (assurance) of something He is saying to us. There are times, as the above Scripture mentions, we'll have an assurance on the inside of us that we are children of God. This is the voice of God. I've heard many believers refer to this kind of assurance as "a check in their spirit." We must pay attention to inner-witnesses that we experience and embrace what God is speaking to us.

I remember soon after giving my life to the Lord, I literally felt saved on the inside of my being. I didn't know why, but all I knew was that I had an assurance in my spirit that I was saved. I would go from friend to friend telling them about the wonderful feeling that I was experiencing. It was awesome as I went through my daily routine with an inside witness that my name was written in the Lamb's book of life. Now, that feeling didn't last forever. It eventually faded as I learned to grab hold of my salvation by faith. Nonetheless, it was a powerful revelation that I cherished as I walked around with a knowledge that I was saved.

Inner witnesses serve a powerful purpose in that they provide a peaceful assurance that God is the One communicating. Be very sensitive to any inner witnesses that you are experiencing. Sometimes, an inner witness could be so gentle, that if you don't teach yourself to be sensitive to your spirit, you won't pick up on it.

As a way to develop that sensitivity, get in the habit of asking yourself, "Do I have a witness about that in my spirit?" That question forces you to look within and notice what's going on inside. Make room so that the candle of the Lord could illuminate with God's inner witness. As you make room for it, God Almighty knows that you're aware of His communication on the inside of you. As a result, you'll see an increase of communication in your spirit man.

Green Light (Go) and Red Light (Stop)

One of the ways that the Holy Spirit communicates within our spirits is to release or stop us. I compare that revelation with what a traffic light does for a car. We look to the traffic lights to dictate to us if we're going to keep driving (green light) or if we're going to stop (red light). Our spirits also receive stop and go communication from the Holy Spirit.

I have had many occasions when I was going to mention something to someone and immediately felt a "stop" in my spirit. It was as if God was on the inside of me telling me not to say it. Many misunderstandings later, I have come to learn that whenever I feel that "stop" in my spirit, no matter how much I want to say it – I bite my tongue. The Holy Spirit will work to prevent us situations of much agony by giving us a "red light" and letting us know when a certain comment would not be appropriate. Learn how to respond!

There are times when I get a "go" in my spirit. I remember on one occasion, I was at church worshipping the Lord. When I saw a friend of mine, I suddenly felt a prophetic unction come over me and I sensed that I was carrying a prophetic word for my friend. Just before I walked over to my friend to download the spiritual message, I quickly checked to see what I was sensing in my sprit. There it was – a "go"! On the inside of my being I had an "assurance" that God indeed wanted me to go and prophesy over my friend. After doing so, my friend confirmed that it was a word that was right on time for him. Praise God. Learn to identify and respond to green lights that the Holy Spirit places in your spirit.

Peace

God is a God of peace. Peace is one of the ways that God will lead us in our spirits.

> *"Be anxious for nothing but in everything, by prayer and supplication, with thanksgiving, let your requests be made known to God; **and the peace of God which surpasses all understanding, will guard your hearts and minds in Christ Jesus**." Philippians 4:6-7 (emphasis mine)*

As you're making your petitions made known to God, be sensitive to the peace that He puts in your spirit. That is a method of His communication to you. On the same note, be aware of a lack of it. If you're looking to make a decision and somehow you notice that there is a lack of peace about the issue – heed the warning!

How many mistakes have we made because we have lacked peace regarding a certain situation and didn't heed the warning? Let's be careful! We have communication from God that takes place in our own being. Let's learn to identify and respond to it.

I remember one situation when I was a lot younger and had my first car. I was driving home from work after a long day. As I was exiting the highway, I noticed that no matter how much I pressed the brakes my car wasn't slowing down on the off-ramp. The brakes weren't responding. I had recently been having problems with the brakes due to the fact that it was an older car. So the event didn't scare me; I knew what to do. My instincts took over and, being that it was winter, I drove my car onto the shoulder of the road and forced my car to run into a mountain of snow. This caused my car to stop instantly. Knowing that I couldn't drive my car without brakes, I decided to leave it on the shoulder of the road and walk the half of a mile to my apartment and call for a tow. Now, it was twilight, and as I was walking on the shoulder of the road heading home, a car pulled up next to me. A young man rolled down his window and kindly offered me a ride. Being that it was very cold, I was ready to say yes and jump into the car. However, I immediately became aware of a lack of peace in my spirit. While at the time I didn't completely know that it was God, I was aware that I didn't feel right about getting into the car. I felt uncomfortable! While the warmth inside of the car seemed appealing to me, I had to heed to this lack of peace that was shouting loudly on the inside of my spirit. I kindly declined the ride and the young man, suddenly looking enraged, raised the window and burned rubber out of there leaving me standing in a cloud of smoke.

I never did understand what was going on with the young man, but I do know that God protected me even from what I couldn't see at the time. Maybe he was driving drunk. Maybe he had drugs on him and was about to be busted by the cops. Maybe the car was stolen. Maybe he had a gun and was looking to take his anger out on someone. I don't know exactly what God protected me from, but I am grateful that He loves me enough that He spoke to me through a lack of peace to prevent me from getting into that car. I learned a valuable lesson about God's communication that day.

There are times when we will suddenly sense a lack of peace regarding someone. It could be our children, siblings, friends, co-workers, etc. This feeling could suddenly overtake us. All we know is that one moment we are fine, and the next moment we have a total lack of peace regarding someone. What should we do?

Firstly, acknowledge what you're feeling. The carnal mind battles against the things of the spirit and will try to get us to "reason" ourselves out of that feeling.

Secondly, ask the Holy Spirit to guide you into all truth. He is the Spirit of Truth and will guide you into all truth. Ask Him to reveal to you why you're feeling that way and how He would like for you to respond.

Thirdly, as you listen to His voice, respond in obedience. Let God lead you in what to do with the lack of peace that you feel. He will show you what to do with it and how to move forward.

Years ago, I was cleaning my home one day when I became aware of a sudden lack of peace that I was feeling. I had a knowing in my spirit that it was regarding my aunt. As I pressed into God for further direction, what I could describe as a cloud of weight came over me and I immediately began to sob and pray in the Holy Spirit. I knew that the Spirit of God was interceding for my aunt through me with groans and expressions that I could not understand.

For thirty minutes I was on the floor helpless as the Spirit of God flowed through me for my aunt. After that time was up, I saw that cloud lift off of me and I was able to get off of the floor, knowing that the time of intercession was over. It was later that week when I learned that my aunt was in a convention in New York City and had suffered a stroke. While she never quite fully recovered, our faith was strengthened during that period of our lives as we observed our aunt continue in her strong faith in the Lord. Today, she's dancing in the presence of the Lord. A lack of peace quickly transitioned into a period of intercession for strength for the family regarding an event that was about to rock us to the core. I believe that as a result of being sensitive to what was going on in my spirit, we were strengthened as my aunt graduated to heaven.

Ask God to Teach You

The purpose of my writing this book is to create an awareness in your life to the voice of God. He is speaking to you in various ways. Activate your senses and respond to Him.

Ask God to teach you how to hear from Him in your spirit. He will be faithful to do so. As you go throughout your day, continue to check back with your spirit to see if you have a sense that was put there by the Holy Spirit. Keep practicing until you can identify those promptings and respond to them.

After activating my spirit to hear from God, I would make sure to check it regularly. Every time I went somewhere for a meeting, I would check my spirit in advance to see if I had communication from God. If someone called me to tell me that they were coming over to my house to talk to me, I would check in my spirit to see if God was putting anything there regarding their visit. The point is that after asking for God's tutelage, you have to do your part to pay attention to your spirit.

Some spirit senses will be strong and pronounced and will immediately capture our attention. Others, however, could be so gentle that an effort has to be made to identify them. Remember the volume button that we talked about. It definitely applies to communication that takes place in our spirits.

Just One Piece of the Puzzle

Communication in our spirits, no matter how gentle or vivid, is just one part of the puzzle. This is just *one* puzzle piece – and we cannot take full action on just one puzzle piece. Remember that you are looking for "two or three witnesses" so that every word can be established.

Once you identify that the Holy Spirit has communicated to you in your spirit man, acknowledge it. Write it down in your journal. If it has something to do with direction for your life (who you're going to marry, what job to accept, which state to move to, e.g.), never move with just one piece of communication. Ask God to confirm it by speaking to you in other ways to confirm what you've heard. By doing that, you remain safe from presumption.

Notes:

1. Jordan S. Rubin, *The Maker's Diet* (Lake Mary:FL: Siloam, 2004) p.51.

- 9 -
A Voice
{Puzzle Piece #4}

"What does God's voice sound like?" is a question I have heard many times. This question is usually asked by some believers who are not sure what to relate the voice of God to.

I usually respond by saying that God's voice is hardly ever a voice. I like to classify His communication as non-verbal and verbal communication. While one of those categories includes non-verbal communication, it is still His voice. If someone waves their hand at you in a greeting, you won't need to hear verbal words to understand that they are saying, "Hello". It is the same concept with God. While God may use non-verbal ways to speak to you, it is still His voice.

Just as God uses non-verbal communication, He also uses verbal communication.

An Audible Voice

That's right! God will still speak through an audible voice today. This is an event that I would consider loud communication on God's volume dial. As I travel in ministry I will usually ask people, during my seminars, to raise their hands if they have heard the audible voice of God. It never ceases to amaze me how many people raise their hands. God still communicates this way.

> *"Then Jesus came from Galilee to John at the Jordan to be baptized by him. And John tried to prevent Him, saying, 'I need to be baptized by You, and are You coming to me?' But Jesus answered and said to him, 'Permit it to be so now, for thus it is fitting for us to fulfill all righteousness.' Then he allowed Him. When He had been baptized, Jesus came up immediately from the water; and behold, the heavens were opened to Him, and He saw the Spirit of God descending like a dove and alighting upon Him. **And suddenly a voice came from heaven, saying, 'This is My beloved Son, in whom I am well pleased.'"** Matthew 3:13-17 (emphasis mine)*

That's right. God's voice thundered from the heavens and spoke about His pleasure over His Son. God confirmed Jesus' identity through an audible voice that spoke from heaven.

Even today, God will at times use His audible voice to speak to us from heaven. We're not to ask God to speak to us this way; we just need to be aware that He can still speak this way today, if He chooses.

A Wake-Up Call

There was a season in my life where God was constantly waking me up at 3:33 a.m. in the morning to pray. (Jeremiah 33:3 – the Scripture that invites us to call unto God for revelation.) I would get up every morning to pray and spend time in the presence of the Lord.

Well, this one morning, I was particularly tired and when I suddenly awoke, I wasn't surprised that the clock read 3:33 a.m. Feeling my exhaustion, I told God, "Lord, I don't want to go downstairs to pray. Please let me pray here on my bed." I started to pray while I was lying in bed. About 1 minute into the prayer, I suddenly began to slip back into a wonderful "sleeper's coma".

Just as I was about to fall into a deep sleep I was suddenly awakened when I heard a loud voice of a man yelling up my stairway, "HELLO!" I sat up in bed with my heart racing. Apparently, I was the only one in the house who heard the voice being that my wife and daughters continued to sleep. While I was shocked to have heard the voice, I wasn't fearful – I felt at peace. Suddenly, a gentle voice spoke to me, and I knew that it was the Holy Spirit. "I'm looking to commune with you."

It was at that moment that I realized that just as I thirst after God, He also longs for me. He desires to commune with me and was inviting me to spend time with Him. I got up from the bed and went down to my living room and did exactly that.

Another thing that I found fascinating was that the voice that I heard sounded exactly like the voice of my best friend. That was no coincidence! God was establishing to me that He is "that friend that sticks closer than a brother". (Proverbs 18:24) Praise God!

Now, if God chooses to speak to you with an audible voice, you'd know it. You wouldn't have to ask yourself if it occurred or not. It's such a loud vivid experience that you would be left with no doubt. While this is a very dramatic way that God chooses to speak today, it's not an event that occurs daily.

Mexico

I already shared with you earlier that my mother received her call to the mission field when God spoke to her audibly. She was awakened around 2 in the morning when a booming-audible voice spoke to her, "You're going to Mexico." While it didn't come to pass until many years later, nonetheless, God was preparing her heart to go and do His will.

An Internal-Audible Voice

There is another way that God uses His voice to speak to us. I stumbled across it when I was a new believer and while I couldn't find a Biblical example that validated it, I've come to realize that we don't know for sure the ways that the prophets heard the word of the Lord. The Bible doesn't always clarify how the word of the Lord came to the prophets. It just may have been an internal-audible voice. Who knows?

Let me define to you what this is. We know that we are temples of the Holy Spirit. So, if I asked you who resides in your spirit, without hesitation you would respond, "The Holy Spirit," which would be a correct answer. Well, the Holy Spirit will at times speak audibly to you, but not to your physical ears, but to the spiritual ears in your spirit.

When this event happens, you hear a voice speaking to you clearly, but you hear it *on the inside of you.* It is different than hearing from God through promptings and sensations in your spirit. This is an actual voice that speaks to you on the inside of your being. All I can say is that like the audible voice of God, you'll know when it happens to you.

An Exhortation to Remain Firm

As I mentioned earlier, I stumbled across this method of

communication as a new believer. I was at a church service one night and I had been serving the Lord for about two months. As the case with all believers, I was just beginning to encounter a series of temptations to return to the old lifestyle I had traded in for Jesus. I was asking God for strength.

At one point in the service, the pastor asked everyone to stand and join in agreement as we said a prayer for one of the members of the congregation. I closed my eyes and joined in agreement with the prayer. As I stood there with my eyes closed, I suddenly heard an audible voice speak on the inside of me. It said, "Do not depart from My ways, for I have great plans for you." I was wowed! Not only was the voice loud and booming, I heard it clearly with ears that I didn't know I had on the inside. I could have plugged my physical ears and still could have heard the voice crisp and clear.

God knew that I was going through various struggles, and He wanted me to stay firm and not to miss out on my destiny in Him. Bless God! As I continued to mature in the Lord, I have encountered many other believers who have also heard the internal-audible voice of God.

People

God will use people to speak through. This also falls under the category of verbal communication. God will regularly communicate His words, guidance and will to us through someone else.

Sermons

Let's not discount that God speaks to us through sermons. When you are listening to a sermon that was designed by the Holy Ghost to speak to you at the point of life where you are at, you have just heard verbal communication from the Father's heart toward you. We need to avoid discounting sermons as a valid method of God's communication.

We will many times look at sermons as "less prophetic" because the minister took time to prepare and is speaking from an outline. However, God knows who will be listening and what they need to hear. So, when a sermon speaks to your heart, don't chalk it up to

mere coincidence – God is behind all communication that speaks
His words to you.

Prophecy

Oh, how wonderful to receive an accurate prophetic word!
There's nothing like it! It really is an experience that fills us with awe
as we ponder God's Sovereignty. There's nothing like knowing that
God knows us and that He knows exactly where we are in life.
Prophetic words will do just that – they will let you hear audible words
from God (from a person's lips) that will give you a motivational boost
to keep moving forward in Him.

> *But he who prophesies speaks edification and exhortation and
> comfort to men." 1 Corinthians 14:3*

Prophecy is that simple! Many people have a misconception of
what prophecy is. Prophecy is basically God sending us to speak to
someone else inspired words of the Holy Ghost for their edification,
exhortation and comfort. God may use a prophet or a prophetic
believer to speak to you. So if you receive a word of prophecy, a
tongue with an interpretation, a word of knowledge or word of wisdom from another person, you are receiving verbal communication
from God the Father.

1 Thessalonians 5:20 says, "Do not despise prophecies." Heed
this exhortation and have an open heart to receive prophetic words
from others. Don't be quick to discount or discard them. Prayerfully
consider them, and embrace the words that are accurate and speak
God's heart to you. Your life will be enhanced as a result of adding
prophecies to your repertoire of hearing from God.

Puzzle Pieces

As you're going through your life being sensitive to God's voice,
be aware of this puzzle piece. God may use an external-audible or
an internal-audible voice to talk to you. Be alert and do the work of a
detective. Journal down anything that the Lord speaks to you through
His voice – do the work of a good detective.

- 10 -
Visions
{Puzzle Piece #5}

I started this book relating an experience that I had when I was 8 years old. It was my first encounter with God. Although at the time I had no idea what a vision was, it was the method that God used to communicate to me at that point in my life.

Let me start out by defining what a vision is. I define a vision as supernatural visual revelation that we see while we are awake. You need to be awake to see a vision – in a complete state of consciousness. While there are revelations that will come at other states of consciousness, they have other names and we'll discuss those in other chapters.

Visions are a major way that God speaks to His people. As you read through the Bible, you'll see that this was a regularly used method by God. Both in the Old and New Testaments, God spoke through visions, and He continues to do so today. As a matter of fact, we know that there is an outpouring of this method of communication because Scripture highlights this.

> "And it shall come to pass in the last days," says God, "that I will pour out of My Spirit on all flesh; your sons and your daughters shall prophesy, your young men **shall see visions**, your old men shall dream dreams." Acts 2:17 (emphasis mine)

Now, you don't have to be a young man to see visions, nor do you have to be an old man to dream dreams. In this Scripture, God highlights the fact that the anointing of the Holy Spirit would be poured out over all ages. Both young and old, sons and daughters, men and women would participate in this great outpouring. That means that this anointing is for you too!

In order to hear from God through visions, we first have to understand the concept behind visions. Visions are a powerful way to hear from God because most humans are visual learners – they learn concepts through visual means. Being that visions fit our learning styles so well, it is an effective way to get a message across to us.

Show and Tell

Visions follow an elementary concept that we learned as children – show and tell.

Many of us remember the day in grade school when we participated in "Show and Tell". For "Show and Tell" all students had to bring something meaningful to school. You may have taken your fuzzy bunny Thumper, and then you had to present him to the class and tell them what Thumper meant to you. So you "showed" the class your item; then you "told" them what it meant to you. Visions follow the same concept. God will reveal (show) us a vision – revelation. He will then reveal (tell) the meaning of the vision – interpretation. After we receive the show and tell, we see the clear picture: revelation and interpretation.

Literal or Symbolic?

Revelations received in visions may reveal something literal or symbolic. When the vision is symbolic, it will require an interpretation from God so that we could have full understanding of its meaning.

In the case of literal visions, God can show you something that's already happened or something that has not yet manifested. The Bible records an example of a literal vision that revealed what was going to happen in the life of Saul of Tarsus shortly after his conversion. When Saul met Jesus on the road to Damascus, he was temporarily blinded; but God was going to take care of that.

> "Now there was a certain disciple at Damascus named Ananias; **and to him the Lord said in a vision, 'Ananias.'** And he said, 'Here I am, Lord.' So the Lord *said* to him, 'Arise and go to the street called Straight, and inquire at the house of Judas **for *one* called Saul of Tarsus, for behold, he is praying. And in a vision he has seen a man named Ananias coming in and putting *his* hand on him, so that he might receive his sight.'** Then Ananias answered, 'Lord, I have heard from many about this man, how much harm he has done to Your saints in Jerusalem.

And here he has authority from the chief priests to bind all who call on Your name.' But the Lord said to him, 'Go, for he is a chosen vessel of Mine to bear My name before Gentiles, kings, and the children of Israel. For I will show him how many things he must suffer for My name's sake.' **And Ananias went his way and entered the house; and laying his hands on him he said, 'Brother Saul, the Lord Jesus, who appeared to you on the road as you came, has sent me that you may receive your sight and be filled with the Holy Spirit.' Immediately there fell from his eyes** *something* **like scales, and he received his sight at once; and he arose and was baptized.** So when he had received food, he was strengthened. Then Saul spent some days with the disciples at Damascus." Acts 9:10-19 (emphasis mine)

God had revealed to Saul a *literal vision* of "a man named Ananias coming and putting his hand on him so that he might receive his sight." That occurred exactly as Saul had seen it in the vision.

This vision needed no interpretation. There was nothing symbolic about what he saw in the vision. As we grow in our ability to hear from God in this way, once we see a vision, one of the first things that we should determine is if the vision is literal or symbolic. If it was literal, we can just journal it in our prophetic journal and let God oversee how it will all come forth. It is not our job to make a revelation come to pass. God reveals to us so that we could know what He is doing; then we trust Him to bring things about in His time and in His way.

You may be asking yourself, "How would I know if the vision is literal or symbolic?" You could usually discern between the two types of visions easily because symbolic visions are much more complex. Symbolic visions also seem more surreal. They require a greater understanding of symbolism and seeking God for interpretations. There are a few key points that will help us develop our ability to understand God's voice in symbolic visions.

#1 – God will use symbolic language that relates to the person.

Symbolic visions will contain…symbols! That's right! God is a Master at using symbols to communicate His will to us. As He uses symbols, we must learn quickly that not all symbols mean the same thing to everybody. Due to our own life experiences, we all carry our own private vocabulary of symbols and our personal belief of their definitions.

Let's look at how the interpretations for a police officer can vary. For a person who has a career goal to enter law enforcement, a police officer may be a positive symbol. For another person who has been mistreated by an officer of the law, a police officer may be to him a negative symbol.

God knows this. God has observed your life from its beginning and knows your feelings toward certain subjects. As the Holy Spirit seeks to communicate to you, if He chooses to speak to you through a symbolic vision, He can just pick through your dictionary of symbols and speak to you using your own symbols.

Jesus did the same thing with the disciples.

> "And Jesus, walking by the Sea of Galilee, saw two brothers, Simon called Peter, and Andrew his brother, **casting a net into the sea; for they were fishermen. Then He said to them, "Follow Me, and I will make you fishers of men."** They immediately left their nets and followed Him. Going on from there, He saw two other brothers, James the son of Zebedee, and John his brother, in the boat with Zebedee their father, mending their nets. He called them, and immediately they left the boat and their father, and followed Him." Matthew 4:18-22 (emphasis mine)

Notice that Jesus used the vocabulary that they were accustomed to. They understood what His calling them meant because they were fishers by trade.

#2 – Develop a symbolic vocabulary.

While God will draw on the symbols that we have already developed through life, He will also begin to give us new symbols. Once the Holy Spirit reveals to you a new symbol, it will be your responsibility to get the mind of God as to its interpretation.

As you retrieve the interpretation of a symbol, I would advise you to keep it in your journal for future purposes. Once God knows that we know the interpretation of a symbol, He may use it with more frequency when we need it.

I remember on one occasion, I was ministering on a prophetic team at a National School of the Prophets to hundreds of people. For two days in a row, for about two hours solid, we would minister to hundreds of people. During that ministry time, a lady approached our team to receive a prophetic word. As we ministered the word of the Lord to her, I could see her drink in the much-needed encouragement. As we concluded the ministry time, this lady turned to leave. Suddenly, as she turned around, I could see many arrows protruding out of her back. It was as if someone was playing target practice on her back. I was shocked to see that. It was the first time that I had ever seen anything like that. In a flash I asked the Holy Spirit to give me the interpretation. Suddenly, I heard the word, "betrayals" in my spirit. Armed with that new knowledge, I asked the lady to come back to us. She walked back toward us curious as to why I was calling her. Then I said, "In Jesus name, I pull out the arrows of betrayal out of your back. For you have been betrayed many times, but God is giving you a balm to heal from those wounds. Move forward in the Lord." When I mentioned the arrows of betrayal, she let out a shout and almost fell to the ground had she not gotten her proper footing. This sister then confirmed the revelation to me by saying, "I have had to walk through many painful betrayals." I could see her countenance change before my very eyes. To God be the glory!

After that event, however, I've seen the "arrows of betrayal" many times on people as I'm ministering prophetically. Most of the time, I'll see the arrows embedded in leaders and pastors. The difference now is that I don't have to press in for an interpretation – I know what it means and how to minister healing from betrayals.

As we mature in hearing from God in visions, on top of being aware of personal symbols, we must cooperate with the Holy Spirit to develop a new vocabulary of symbols.

#3 – Interpretations belong to God.

As Anointed Detectives, our job is not to interpret the new symbols, but to ask God for their meaning.

"Do not interpretations belong to God?" Genesis 40:8

If you've read a book and wanted to know what the author meant by a certain expression, who would be the best person to ask? That's right – the author. Only the author can truly clarify the meaning of what they've expressed. In the same way, who would be the best person to interpret the God-given vision that you saw? Being that the Holy Spirit is the author of the vision, He would be the best One to interpret it.

In today's age, we want everything now. We want all things of value to be dropped onto our laps without too much effort on our part. That is the same attitude that we bring to hearing the voice of God. We want God to immediately reveal to us revelation, and then immediately give us the meaning and the application. This kind of lifestyle promotes a lack of self-discipline, and the person will never develop his full prophetic potential.

This attitude has caused some believers to abuse symbol dictionaries. They want the understanding to their dreams and visions and they want it now. They are not willing to learn how to press in to God for interpretations. Rather, the quick fix is to look up the interpretation in a symbol dictionary.

Now, I'm not criticizing symbol dictionaries. They serve a very helpful purpose. I know that some people have a tough challenge thinking symbolically and these dictionaries will be of great help to them. What I am saying is that laziness causes us to abuse the purpose for these dictionaries. Then we're upset when we don't see the fruit of the revelation in our lives. The dictionaries are great to help get us started, but then we must learn to work with the Holy Spirit to hear from Him what the symbols mean. God wants us to get to the place where we look to Him for interpretations, not a dictionary.

I've heard people rattle off "meanings" of symbols from their dictionaries interpreting everyone else's visions. They say, "Well, it says here that the green represents envy and the car represents your ministry and then this represents that...." Give me a break! Quit running to the owner of the dictionary to help you with an interpretation. Learn to wait on the Lord and allow Him to interpret your symbols for you. After all, if He gave you the vision, He is the author of the symbol and would really know its meaning. Then when you believe that you've received an interpretation, ask God to give you a confirmation so that you could walk with assurance. He'll be faithful to let you know if you got it or missed it.

So, here are two methods to help you learn how to receive an interpretation from God:

Method 1 — Look at the symbol and ask God to give you the meaning. Be silent before Him and give Him the opportunity to give you insight. Write down all of the promptings and impressions that come your way. You need to be open to all of the other ways He speaks to bring you an interpretation.

Method 2 — Ponder on the symbol to see what it could mean. Get in the habit of thinking symbolically. Just like any skill, this skill gets perfected with time. Keep going over the symbol in your mind, asking yourself what it could mean. Like a detective, look at the symbol from all angles and ask yourself all the necessary questions to get the interpretation. As you ponder the symbol, you'll recognize when you arrive at a God-given interpretation. The light bulb will go on above your head, and you'll get an "AHA" moment. You may even feel a witness in your spirit as you get the interpretation.

Confirmations – Now remember, the whole purpose of this book is to encourage God's people to press in for confirmations. Once you believe that you have the interpretation of a symbolic vision, if it has anything to do with direction for your life, ask God for 2 or 3 witnesses to confirm the revelation. Make sure to document the ways that God speaks to you and what He says. Also, make sure to capture the dates of when God spoke to you. Having the dates is helpful when we look back to see how long God has been talking to us about a matter. Any revelation that God sends your way that requires change of direction for your life, you should have enough confirmations to prove that God has been speaking to you. Only one piece of revelation is *not* enough to make changes in your life. Make sure that you are not walking in presumption. Get those confirmations.

#4 – You can develop your ability to see visions.

No, that statement is not a blasphemy. You can truly develop your ability to see visions. Many believers come from the school of thought that, "if God wants to give me a vision, He can give me a vision." That statement while true, represents the believer who thinks that God *always* has to bring a vision to them. God will speak to you in a vision when He wants to speak to you in that way! There is, however, another part to the equation.

Just as God can send you the "word of the Lord," you can also *go* to the "word of the Lord." What that means is that you could develop your spiritual eyes to be in a constant state of "watching" for visions from God. Let's look at an example from the Bible.

> **"I will stand upon my watch, and set me upon the tower, and will watch to see what he will say unto me, and what I shall answer when I am reproved**. And the LORD answered me, and said, **Write the vision, and make it plain upon tables, that he may run that readeth it. For the vision is yet for an appointed time, but at the end it shall speak, and not lie: though it tarry, wait for it; because it will surely come, it will not tarry."**
> Habakkuk 2:1-3 (King James Version — emphasis mine)

The prophet was complaining and spending time seeking the Lord for some answers regarding His people. As he was praying, he was "standing on his watch on the tower, watching to see what God would say unto him". Habakkuk didn't wait for God to bring the vision to him. On the contrary, he was constantly watching to see. What was the result? In a vision, God revealed to the prophet what would happen and then told him to write it down and to make it plain. The vision came as a result of Habukkuk's constant praying and watching.

If we would take on that same determination, we would be able to develop spiritual eyes that see everything that God sends our way. I would like for you to imagine a huge, tall, steel door. Let's say that this door is the door to God's revelation. God's children are used to standing outside of this door and waiting for it to open. Their mentality is, "Well, whatever God wants me to have, He'll open the door and give it to me." So they wait outside of the door for providential revelation to be handed to them. God in His goodness knows what they need and will bring them much of the needed revelation. However, they are not going to receive all of what God has for them because remember, "God loves a seeker." No, He doesn't mind bringing us revelation. However, He is pleased when His children are so hungry to hear from Him that they are constantly banging on the door saying, "God, I need to hear from You." You don't have to wait for God to bring it to you; you can develop a lifestyle of banging on the door of revelation from God and live in expectation to receive from Him. This change of attitude will create in you the attitude of a seeker.

So now, we're developing spiritual eyes to see visions from God. We have told God that we want our eyes to be used by Him and that we want to see anything that He wants to show us. What else can we do to develop our spiritual sight?

First I would advise you to practice looking to see what God shows you. What this basically means is when you're spending time in the presence of God, before closing your prayer and leaving, get used to being still before God to hear from Him. Have expectation that He will speak to you. As you are still before Him, close your eyes and meditate on the Lord. Continue to ask yourself, "Am I seeing anything?" By asking yourself this question you are forcing yourself to look to see if a vision is being revealed to you. Not all visions are vivid and some are so gentle in nature that if you don't focus on it, you can miss it.

Second of all, I would advise you to practice using your spiritual eyes when you pray for someone. We will usually have friends and family ask us for prayer and in our tradition of prayer, we tend to close our eyes and tell God what to do in their lives. Let's shift from that mindset to letting the Holy Spirit speak to us what He wants us to pray. Rather than rushing in with prayer, take a moment to be silent to hear what God is speaking to you. Remember to look with your spiritual eyes to see if God is revealing anything to you. By purposely using your eyes, you are training yourself to use your spiritual sight to see what God would show you. Once God sees that you are being purposeful in developing your spiritual sight and are standing on your watch to see what He will say to you, like Habukkuk, you will hear His voice with greater frequency because you are being intentional.

#5 – There are many different kinds of visions.

Visions range in vividness and how they are seen. We have

already established the concept of God's volume button. This applies also to visions. Another quote that I hear a lot is, "I know it was from God because it was so vivid." By saying that, we disqualify the less vivid revelations that come our way. Remember, God may speak to you vividly or softly. We are not to judge the communication by the vividness but by the message.

Visions also vary in the way that they are seen. We must know the various ways that they are revealed to us so that we could be ready to grasp God's words to us. Let's go into the various categories.

Impressions

These visions are lower on the volume channel because they are very soft in nature. These impressions are easy to throw out and ignore because of how gentle they are in nature.

An impression vision is a very faint picture that you may see with your eyes open or closed. The picture that you see may be fuzzy, black and white, or different shades of gray. These are less pronounced pictures and again are easy to ignore. If you see an impression, don't throw it out immediately. Journal it and ask God for the interpretation and look to see how it fits your life.

I never paid any attention to impressions that I had seen while in prayer. God set me up on one occasion to catch my attention. The first time that I ministered on a prophetic team, I was very nervous. There was a team of four of us ministering to a congregation of people one by one from the front of the church. We had just gone down a line of people and were in the process of ministering to a woman from our church that I didn't know. While the other two or three people were ministering prophetically to her, I couldn't seem to get anything from God. I began to panic being that I was next in line to speak prophetically and I couldn't seem to get anything from God. Suddenly, I saw an impression of a snowflake. Just as I saw it, I was handed the microphone. Normally, I would have ignored such a vision because it was so faint. Since it was all I had, however, I decided to tell her what I was seeing. As I was going to tell her the impression that I saw, suddenly the interpretation hit my spirit. With great boldness and authority I said to her, "Just like there are no two snowflakes alike, the Lord says that you are unique. Your calling and anointing are unique, and you are called by Him to a unique task that only you can do." The lady smiled, and I could see that the word greatly blessed her. I found out much later that the lady was a missionary to Colombia and that the prophetic word encouraged her regarding her call since she was just getting ready to go back to the mission field.

I was also encouraged to learn that the revelation came to me in the form of a faint impression. Since then, I quit throwing the impressions out and I began to pay attention to them. Today, I continue to receive impressions from God and they have brought such powerful revelations to me, just like any other valid way that God speaks. Don't ignore the impressions!

I have a friend who heard me teach on this concept once. I was teaching on all the various ways that God speaks and as I covered visions, I gave the exhortation not to ignore impressions. Shortly afterward, I was ministering in a church in Buffalo, New York, and invited this friend to come along with me. After prophesying over many in the church, I called the pastors forward so that we could give them the word of the Lord. After I was done prophesying, I gave my friend the opportunity to also speak over this pastor and his wife, and I was amazed with the powerful word that he declared. Afterward, the pastor thanked my friend for such an accurate word. On the drive home, I congratulated my friend for giving such an accurate word and asked him how he received the revelation from God. He told me that God showed him a vision and it came in the form of an impression. He said, "Hector, it was so faint that I almost didn't pay attention to it. However, I remember when you taught us not to ignore impressions, so I asked God for the interpretation and that's when He gave me that accurate word for them." I was so happy that my friend added another powerful tool of hearing God's voice to his repertoire.

Internal Visions

We all have what is referred to as "the mind's eye" due to the fact that our minds think in pictures. Every time we are having a conversation with someone, as they are talking to us, our minds are forming the pictures in our imagination center so that we could envision what they're saying to us.

Let's test out this concept. Okay, reader, what I would like for you to do right now is to picture a white puppy with big brown spots. Were you able to see the puppy? I'm sure you were. Why? Because our minds think in pictures. When I gave you the suggestion of what to see, you pictured it in your mind's eye or in your imagination center.

Now in the example above, I told you what to picture – the puppy. That is what is referred to as "visualization". This is what the world practices when they conduct business empowerment seminars and tell the people to "visualize" themselves as successful, happy, and powerful. If you visualize something, that does not mean that you're having a God-inspired vision. It just means that you are putting suggestions into your mind's eye.

An internal vision occurs when *the Holy Spirit* is the one who puts the picture into your mind's eye. How do you know the difference? Well, it all boils down to who put the picture there. If you desire to go on vacation and are having images flash in your mind's eye about white sandy beaches, blue waters or tiki torches, then you can be sure that you are visualizing your desires. However, if you are going about your day and suddenly a picture flashes in your mind's eye about a friend you haven't seen in a while, and suddenly later that day you run into that friend, I would say you probably had an internal vision. Don't misunderstand me; I'm not saying that by visualizing something you are sinning. Not at all. God made our minds to function that way. What I am saying is that we have to be sensitive to the pictures that flash in our mind's eye that we did not put there. We have to discern to see if it would fit God's communication, and then move forward with it if it is from God.

These are visions that are also lower on the volume level; nonetheless, they are powerful revelations from God. It is rare that I don't see an internal vision every time I'm ministering prophetically to people. The Lord uses them quite frequently to speak to us. The faster we recognize this form of communication, the quicker we could enjoy the benefit of God's insight.

The enemy also wants to influence this imagination center. As believers we have to protect our mind's eye from pictures that try to float in as a result of the enemy's suggestions. We have all had to rebuke mental images of choking an annoying relative or coworker. We have all had to rebuke images of fear when we are about to do something big for the first time like preach in front of a crowd or travel in an airplane. The imagination center is a powerful weapon that God can use for His glory, but we must sanctify it for His use and do our part to keep it clean.

Closed Visions

Basically, a closed vision is a vision that we see while our eyes are closed. It's amazing how our spiritual eyes work, even when our physical eyelids are closed. This is the way that I saw the vision when I was 8 years old. While my eyes were closed, it looked like a huge screen opened up before me and I was able to see a slideshow of pictures. In a closed vision, you may see only one picture, various pictures, or a movie-like scene playing.

When you are being still before the Lord, close your eyes and watch to see if your spiritual eyes will capture a closed vision. We don't fabricate visions or make them happen; however, we can practice looking and watching to see what He will say to us. By practicing, we are developing habits that will assist us in developing a seer's anointing.

Open Visions

Well, if a closed vision is what is seen when your eyes are closed, then an open vision is when your eyes are opened. Like a closed vision, in an open vision God may reveal to you a picture, several pictures, or a movie-like scene.

As a new believer, my mother had an open vision of a pastor-friend's ministry. This pastor-friend of my mother had just launched out and started a new church. They had been friends for a while and she was committed to praying for him and his new ministerial venture. Shortly afterward, my mother was traveling to a church convention on a Greyhound bus. As she settled into her seat on the bus, she was shocked when she saw her pastor-friend standing in the aisle of the bus. Not realizing it was a vision, she asked him, "What are you doing here?" He didn't respond and she watched in horror as he slowly continued to lean forward until he fell on the floor of the bus and broke into many little pieces. My mother, being a new believer, didn't know what to do with such a revelation and decided to keep it to herself and just to cover it in prayer. Months later, she wasn't surprised to hear that her pastor-friend had given up his church because it didn't work out for him. She had received that knowledge beforehand in an open vision from God as to how the ministry venture wouldn't work out. Now, some of you may think, "That was the enemy who wanted to stop the pastor's ministry." We must remember that we need to be sure that it's God's voice that we're hearing and following as we start out in ministry. If we launch out for any other reason, it's sure to be a failure.

If while you are praying, the Lord Jesus Christ walks into your room and begins to communicate with you, you are having an open vision. Or if you are in your church and notice an angel walk in, you are having an open vision. Open visions are revelations that we see when our eyes are open.

Higher Level Visions

The Lord also uses higher-level visions to reveal His will to His children. These visions are higher on the volume dial. When they occur, God is not whispering but "shouting" forth His revelation.

Trances – Don't panic! Many of you see this word and you immediately think of psychics and fortune-tellers. Trances were designed by God as a high-level revelation to speak to His children. Remember, Satan is the master counterfeiter. He copied God's invention and uses trances in his kingdom of darkness to speak to his servants. Just because the enemy copied it, doesn't disqualify trances as a valid method of communication from God.

A trance is a high-level vision in which you are taken to another dimension and are revealed something by the Holy Spirit. Peter was caught up into a trance while he was praying on the rooftop.

> *"The next day, as they went on their journey and drew near the city, Peter went up on the housetop to pray, about the sixth hour. Then*

*he became very hungry and wanted to eat; but while they made
ready, **he fell into a trance and saw** heaven opened and an object
like a great sheet bound at the four corners, descending to him and
let down to the earth. In it were all kinds of four-footed animals of
the earth, wild beasts, creeping things, and birds of the air. And a
voice came to him, 'Rise, Peter; kill and eat.' But Peter said, "Not
so, Lord! For I have never eaten anything common or unclean."
Acts 10:9-14 (emphasis mine)*

We need to cultivate an atmosphere for God to speak to us in
whatever way He sees fit. If He wants to speak to us in a trance, we
must be ready to be open to it. While we don't look for trances to
happen, we need to be aware that God may decide to communicate
to us through one. God used a trance once to get me to repent for
being a lukewarm Christian.

When I was a new believer, I went through a season of my
Christian life where I was beginning to slowly grow cold. Throughout
this season, God was reaching out to me through various ways
warning me to get right. Unfortunately, no matter how much I received the warnings, I couldn't seem to muster up the motivation to
get my walk right with God and continued my drift away from Him.

One night as I was getting ready to go to sleep, I was caught up
into a trance. As soon as my head touched the pillow, I was somewhere else, and the scenery around me changed. Without warning, I
suddenly found myself laying on a gurney in a hospital. There were a
bunch of doctors around the gurney looking down at me and they
were running with my bed, wheeling me down the hallway. It was a
moment of panic. I heard over the loudspeakers a voice saying,
"Code Red, Code Red." As I looked up from the gurney at the doctors, I could tell that something was completely wrong. I was terri-
fied. I started shouting, "What's wrong? What's going on?" Then I
heard one doctor begin to yell at the others, "We're losing him!
We're losing him!" With that, I fell into a deep sleep and didn't wake
up until the next morning. When I remembered the trance, it put the
fear of God into me, and I immediately repented for my being lukewarm and got my heart right with the Lord. I recognized that the
vision was symbolic and was a warning from God that I was at a
point where my spiritual life was in danger due to my walking away
from Him. I am so grateful for that revelation that caused me to

respond to the voice of the Lord and rededicate myself to Him.

When trances occur, the person may still be physically in the same place he was when it overtook him. For example, if you are praying at the altar and you are taken into a trance, although you are somewhere in a spiritual dimension seeing visions, everyone else can still see your physical body at the altar. People have been known to go into trances when they fall under the power of the Spirit. I've heard people get up later from the floor and say, "I was gone some-where else." Although the person was in a spiritual realm, his body was still very much in the physical realm.

Being Caught Up – These are high-level visions where God will visit us to commune or to reveal His word to us.

> "After these things I looked, and behold, a door standing open in heaven. And the first voice which I heard was like a trumpet speaking with me, saying, '**Come up here, and I will show you things which must take place after this.' Immediately I was in the Spirit; and behold, a throne set in heaven, and *One* sat on the throne**." Revelation 4:1-2 (emphasis mine)

These are different from other visions in that not only are you revealed a vision, you are taken physically into the vision.

Several years ago, I met a man of God who constantly received high-level revelations. Being that we lived in opposite sides of the country, our visits were limited to phone conversations. Every time I would call him, he would share with me about a new revelation that God gave him for the Body of Christ. I was amazed at how much the Holy Spirit would give me a confirmation about how valid these revelations were. One day, this brother told me that he was in the living room praying when suddenly he was taken and found himself standing in a library in heaven. God began to give him much insight as to what takes place in that room. When he came back to his living room, he looked at the clock and was amazed that he was gone for over an hour. Shortly afterward, his wife walked past him, and he asked her if she had seen him in the chair. She responded and told him that she had been in the living room quite a bit and that he wasn't there. She just assumed that he was outside watering the lawn. Well, it was confirmed to him that he had just experienced a visitation. He was physically taken into that library room in heaven and given a powerful revelation. Praise God!

When it's an open vision, your eyes are open and you are behold-ing a vision. When it's a trance, you are taken into a spiritual realm and given a vision, even though your body stays put. When you are caught up, you are taken completely into the vision. Just like in the above Scripture, John saw a door in heaven and then heard a voice inviting him to come up to heaven. The Bible says that suddenly he was in the Spirit and was standing in heaven. Through this visitation, John was able to record the book or Revelation that gives us the idea of how things will conclude here on this earth.

The Seer Anointing

Regardless of the type of vision and the volume level, visions are incorporated into the seer anointing. Our focus is not to make a certain type of vision manifest, but to keep our spiritual eyes open so that we could flow in the seer anointing.

In the Old Testament, the prophet was called "Seer". This was because as they inquired of the Lord, one of the major ways that God communicated to them was through visions.

> *"Formerly in Israel, when a man went to inquire of God, he spoke thus: Come, let us go to the seer; for he who is now called a prophet was formerly called a seer." 1 Samuel 9:9*

Today, you don't have to be a prophet to develop the "seer anoint-ing". Remember that God promised that He would be pouring His Spirit upon all of His children to see visions in the last days. If the Lord Jesus Christ is your Lord and Savior, you can develop the seer anointing and walk in it.

Ask the Holy Spirit to work with you on developing the "seer anointing". He'll be faithful to do so.

One Piece of the Puzzle

Remember that visions, no matter what kind or what volume, are one piece of the puzzle. God will usually give more than one witness to you when it comes to revelations that bring direction for your life.

Keep in mind that as an Anointed Detective, your job is to continue to collect the clues that give you a *clear* picture of what God is saying to you. Once God reveals something to you in a vision, journal it, then ask Him to confirm it to you through other ways. Keep your eyes and ears open and look for God because His confirmations to us are sure.

-11 -
Dreams
{Puzzle Piece #6}

The Dream of the Disappointed Visitor

I was going through a rough phase of life while I was completing my college degree. Work, school, family and ministry were all beginning to take a toll on me as I found myself buried underneath mounds of responsibilities.

One area that I always had to battle was worry. I was *always* worrying about something. I worried that I wasn't doing a good enough job at work. Then, I worried that I wasn't making enough money to make ends meet. On top of that, I struggled to see how we were going to make our next payments on our bills. I worried about the future. On and on it went; a lifestyle of continual worry. The problem was that I never knew I was doing anything wrong. After all, I was the head of the household and the priest of my home. Wasn't that my job?

Spiritually, I thought everything was going fine in my life. Although I constantly felt overwhelmed with my daily responsibilities, I knew I could "do everything through Christ who strengthens me." I knew that I battled with worry, but I also believed that God knew that I was doing my best – so I was okay with Him.

One night I went to sleep and had a very vivid dream. In this dream, I was in my living room pacing. I was worrying about something. I was asking myself questions aloud that had to do with how I was going to meet my responsibilities. I saw myself wringing my hands as I paced the room worrying. My worry session immediately got interrupted as I heard the footsteps of someone coming down the stairs. I could tell that whoever was coming down the stairs was upset because they were stomping loudly on each step. I stood there wondering who would be coming down the stairs in that fashion when suddenly I saw Him. He had a long white robe with shoulder-length brown hair. It was Jesus! I could see everything clear except His face – it was blurry. He came down the stairs so fast and walked toward me so quickly that I didn't have time to adjust to the fact that I was seeing Jesus. Upon seeing Him, every hair on my body stood on end. He quickly approached me and without saying one word, He reached out and grabbed both of my hands in His hands. He grabbed them aggressively and just held my hands without saying a word. Although He didn't speak, I sensed that He was making a point clear to me. As He stood there holding my hands, I quickly noticed that they started burning. They were burning so strong that I almost began to yell out from the pain. Suddenly, I woke up and realized it was a dream. I also noticed that my hands continued to burn even after being awake.

When I woke up, I was in awe because I had the sense that I was just visited by Jesus in a dream. I really didn't need much of an interpretation to understand what God was saying to me. He was telling me that He wanted me to understand the concept once and for all that He is not pleased with worry and anxiety. That is why the word says:

> "And do not seek what you should eat or what you should drink, nor have an anxious mind." Luke 12:29

> "Be anxious for nothing, but in everything by prayer and supplication, with thanksgiving, let your requests be made known to God..." Philippians 4:6

God used this dream to speak to me about my need to repent for worrying. In my folly, I had ascribed worrying to my duty as the breadwinner of the house. God was correcting that false concept and confirming to me that every time I worry, I am deliberately choosing not to trust Him.

Oh, how I thank God that one of the ways that He speaks to us is through dreams. Hearing the voice of God in dreams is very important for the many reasons that I'm about to explain. But first, let me define what a dream is.

I define a dream as something that you see when you're asleep. That's the key with dreams: you have to be asleep to have them. I usually get asked the difference between dreams and visions. The answer to this is very easy: with a dream you are asleep; with a vision you are awake.

In concept, dreams are very similar to visions. They also:

~are a part of the seer's anointing

~follow the "show and tell" format
(revelation and interpretation)

~could be literal or symbolic

~vary in their vividness (volume)

Dreams Can Reach a Closed Heart

One of the most important aspects of hearing from God in dreams is that God can reach a closed heart. There are various reasons why we are usually closed off to God's voice.

1 – We reason away God's voice.

You see, all of the other ways in which God speaks deal with us while we are awake. It is also while we are awake that our natural minds are more active. We already know that the carnal mind always fights against the things of the Spirit because the mind cannot comprehend the things of the Sprit. As a result, whenever God chooses His other methods to speak to us, there is a possibility that we may ignore or reason away the Spirit's revelation to us.

There have been many times after I have seen a vision from the Lord that my carnal mind kicks in and starts convincing me that I didn't see anything – that I made it all up. Other times when the Holy Spirit had given me a prompting in my spirit, my carnal mind fought against it and told me that I really didn't feel anything. To be sensitive to the voice of God and to hear from Him in all of the ways He speaks means that we have to constantly battle and subject a carnal mind that wants to disregard God's communication.

As God's children, it is possible that we may enter into areas of deception because we have reasoned away God's revelation to us. For example, let's say that God had been speaking to you to get more involved in your local church. Your carnal mind starts fighting against the revelations coming to you, and you come to the conclusion that you are making it all up because you feel guilty that you haven't been involved more. So you disregard all prior revelation that has been sent to you. You are now in a place outside of God's will for your life. What you need is to hear from God in a way that will allow you to hear directly from Him by bypassing your carnal mind and not give it an opportunity to fight the revelation. God-given dreams will do exactly that.

This doesn't imply that the other ways that God speaks to us are inferior to dreams. We don't have to be asleep to hear the accurate voice of God. With time, we learn how to subject the carnal mind to God's revelation so that we are not throwing out valid communication. Dreams, however, fit perfectly into our "hearing God" repertoire because if we missed something that God was saying to us, we have a powerful method that God can use to bypass our active minds and confront us with truth.

I was once offered the opportunity to submit my name for consideration as the President of a Board of Directors at a local community-based organization that meant a lot to me. I politely asked the person to give me a few days to consider the offer. I was going to ask the Lord about His will for me in this situation. I was quite flattered that I was one of the candidates being considered and had a strong bent towards going for it. Even though I kept getting a dull sense in my spirit, I attributed that feeling to being nervous of actually functioning in such a position. (On other occasions, this dull sense was a way the Holy Spirit would tell me "no" as an answer. I didn't discern that sense as a "no" because I really wanted to have this position). I had become entrapped by my heart's desire and was at the point that I was convincing myself that God wanted me to do this.

Our souls, if they are not surrendered, can be very manipulative to get their way. This had become so subtle that I didn't even realize that I was reasoning away all of the direction that God was sending to me. Finally, I had a dream one night in which I was at the organization and I was observing myself working with the employees of the agency. I was shocked to see how badly we were working together. As I woke up from the dream I heard the phrase, "wrong relationship". With that dream, God bypassed my heart's desire and spoke to me about why this wasn't His will for me. He warned me that if I was to go ahead and get involved, I was in danger of getting out of His will and developing a soul tie with this agency. I called the person who asked me to consider the opportunity and politely declined the offer. Shortly afterward, I was relieved of my decision as I became aware of certain information that was withheld from me. Had I gone for it and was elected as the president of the board, I would have later regretted it and would have been in a very ugly situation. Oh, how I praise God that He loved me so much that He bypassed my desires and revealed His truth to me.

2 – We are not aware that God is speaking to us.

> "For God may speak in one way, or in another, yet man does not perceive it. In a dream, in a vision of the night, when deep sleep falls upon men, while slumbering on their beds. Then He opens the ears of men, and seals their instruction." Job 33:14-16

There are those who go through life oblivious that God is speaking to them. The above Scripture confirms that. However, even these disconnected Christians are not out of God's reach. God may certainly change the way in which He is reaching out to them so that they can also be confronted with God's truths. Dreams are usually the language that God chooses to speak to break through barriers of unawareness, unbelief or deception.

The above Scripture explains the fact that while man does not perceive God's voice, He'll wait for him/her to fall asleep and then open their ears to seal their instruction. Why open their ears? You only open ears that are closed. I find it amazing that in the days in which we live, people actually go through life with their spiritual ears and eyes closed. While we all can benefit from hearing God in dreams, these are people that especially need to learn how to do it to help them with their spiritual hearing problem.

Dream Rules to Live By

There is a correct way to hear from God in dreams that will result in us bearing fruit in our lives. There is an incorrect way to pay attention to dreams that will result in frustration and lack of growth. If we are going to hear God's voice, we'll need to make sure we are going about it in the correct way.

1 – 95% of our dreams are about you the individual.

I know that some of you are going to have a hard time with this concept. We are so used to running around and telling everyone the dreams we had with them in it. That just displays our ignorance as far as how dreams operate.

Let me ask you a question. If your pastor wanted to speak into your personal life, would you prefer if he spoke it to me so that I could tell it to you, or would you prefer that your pastor speak to you directly? You would rather that he delivered it to you directly! I would also prefer that. You would not want me to be a "meddler" in the information that your pastor wants to tell you. After all, I may divulge the information to third and fourth parties. Or I may forget to tell you and therefore wait until it's too late to give you the message. Lastly, I'm sure that you would appreciate the confidentiality of your pastor sharing that delicate information directly with you alone. Why then, if we would like that kind of consideration, do we think that God would give us all of these dreams about other people's business so that we could know it? Think about that. God will usually speak to a person directly about his own life.

"But brother Hector, what about prophets? What about prophecy?" you ask. God can and will use the prophetic to speak to encourage us and to use it as a puzzle piece to add to our own hearing. He will not divulge all of your information to another person at your church who has no reason for knowing anything about your life, except if they may have a prophetic gift and God is using them to encourage you. Even then, they won't know all of your information and they won't have daily revelation for you. God will speak to you about you.

When it comes to a ministry, in like manner, God will usually establish a direct line of communication with the person overseeing the ministry. God deals with the person that He has put in authority and will speak to them. He will use other vessels to bring revelation and confirming words, but not all the time. Here are some examples of how God speaks to the person in authority:

~ God will speak to an Apostle about the church networks he oversees.

~ God will speak to a Prophet about revelation for the Body of Christ.

~ God will speak to an Evangelist about where and how to win souls.

~ God will speak to a Pastor about the church he pastors.

 ~ God will speak to a Teacher about revelation from the Scriptures.

~ God will speak to a Husband / Wife about their household and children.

~ God will speak to Employers about their businesses and employees.

~ God will speak to a Ministry Leader about the ministry he oversees.

~ God will speak to a person about direction for his / her life.

Do you see how God does this? We must all know where God has called us and what authority we have.

Now that we understand that God always deals directly with individuals that He puts in authority, let's look at a misconception that this will help clear up.

Intercessors: Not all of your dreams are for your church!

I have encountered too many intercessors who believe that because they pray for their church, every dream that they have is about the church. Then, as they share their dreams with the Pastor, if he doesn't take immediate action on that revelation, they become offended.

Now please don't misunderstand me. Intercessors are very much needed and have a special place in the Body of Christ. I am in no way minimizing all the wonderful tasks that you are undertaking for our Lord. It's just that some have unfortunately fallen into a major trap of not believing that their dreams are God's voice for their own lives. If we are giving all our dreams to our pastors as a prophetic word for our church, we are being irresponsible. At no time can one intercessor become the official "word receiver" for the church so that every dream that they have is for the church. Through your dreams, God wants to talk to *you* about *you*. Here's a good rule of thumb for intercessors: Apply all dreams to yourself first before applying it to the church. You'll be amazed how much you thought was for your church is actually for your own life.

Now if you are an intercessor for your church, will God speak to you for the church? Sure He will. However, we need to understand how to receive confirmations on the messages that we pass on to leadership. We must be responsible enough to test all revelation. With dreams, it is required that we understand they are vehicles in which God will mostly speak to us for our own lives.

My advice to intercessors is that if you believe that God gave you a dream for the church and you have the interpretation of the dream, ask God to use another way that He speaks to confirm that prophetic word to you before submitting it. This is helpful especially when we just wake up from a dream and the dream is still very vivid to us. When the dream is still fresh, we usually feel that we have to hurry up and share its content and message. By waiting for a confirma-tion, you are allowing time for the dream to cool off and with it, any emotional attachment to immediately share the message. It's more substantial to your leaders whenever you do share revelation to not only have a dream and its interpretation, but also other puzzle pieces that confirm what you have heard. This makes the revelation more credible.

2 – 95% of our dreams are symbolic in nature!

The majority of dreams that we read about in the Bible were symbolic. When Joseph dreamed about the sheaves of wheat, the stars, moon and sun bowing to him, it had nothing to do with sheaves of wheat or the celestial bodies. These dreams were symbolic in nature and through them, God was speaking to Joseph about the leadership role he would step into in the future. If we took this literally, we would assume that Joseph saw sheaves of wheat bowing to him in the fields and the sun, moon and stars bowing in outer space. No, it was a symbolic message to Joseph for Joseph.

When Pharaoh dreamed about seven fat cows and seven skinny cows coming up from the Nile River, the dream had nothing to do with cows. Pharaoh's second dream of seven healthy heads of grain coming from one stalk and seven measly heads of grain had nothing to do with grain. This was a symbolic dream. Each fat cow represented a year of abundance and each skinny cow a year of famine. The fat ones came up out of the river first followed by the skinny ones, meaning that there would be seven years of abundance and then seven of famine. The fact that they came out of the river represents that it was something being brought forth of the Lord. (Rivers usually represent something that the Holy Spirit is doing.) Through this symbolic dream, God gave Pharaoh a picture of what was to come. Notice that there was some time in between having the dream and understanding the meaning. In order to benefit from God-given dreams, we must develop the skill of interpreting symbols. Let's look at what happened after Pharaoh had the dream.

> *"Now it came to pass in the morning that his (Pharaoh's) spirit was troubled, and he sent and called for all the magicians of Egypt and all its wise men. And Pharaoh told them his dreams, but there was no one who could interpret them for Pharaoh. Then the chief butler spoke to Pharaoh, saying, 'I remember my faults this day. When Pharaoh was angry with his servants, and put me in custody in the house of the captain of the guard, both me and the chief baker, we each had a dream in one night, he and I. Each of us dreamed according to the interpretation of his own dream. Now there was a young Hebrew man with us there, a servant of the captain of the guard. And we told him, and he interpreted our dreams for us; to each man he interpreted according to his own dream. And it came to pass, just as he interpreted for us, so it happened. He restored me to my office, and he hanged him.' Then Pharaoh sent and called Joseph, and they brought him quickly out of the dungeon; and he shaved, changed his clothing, and came to Pharaoh. And Pharaoh said to Joseph, 'I have had a dream, and there is no one who can interpret it. But I have heard it said of you that you can understand a dream, to interpret it.' So Joseph answered Pharaoh, saying, 'It is not in me; God will give Pharaoh an answer of peace.' Then Pharaoh said to Joseph: 'Behold, in my dream I stood on the bank of the river. Suddenly seven cows came up out of the river, fine looking and fat; and they fed in the meadow. Then behold, seven*

other cows came up after them, poor and very ugly and gaunt, such ugliness as I have never seen in all the land of Egypt. And the gaunt and ugly cows ate up the first seven, the fat cows. When they had eaten them up, no one would have known that they had eaten them, for they were just as ugly as at the beginning. So I awoke. Also I saw in my dream, and suddenly seven heads came up on one stalk, full and good. Then behold, seven heads, withered, thin, and blighted by the east wind, sprang up after them. And the thin heads devoured the seven good heads. So I told this to the magicians, but there was no one who could explain it to me.' **Then Joseph said to Pharaoh, 'The dreams of Pharaoh are one; God has shown Pharaoh what He is about to do: The seven good cows are seven years, and the seven good heads are seven years; the dreams are one. And the seven thin and ugly cows which came up after them are seven years, and the seven empty heads blighted by the east wind are seven years of famine.** *This is the thing which I have spoken to Pharaoh. God has shown Pharaoh what He is about to do. Indeed seven years of great plenty will come throughout all the land of Egypt; but after them seven years of famine will arise, and all the plenty will be forgotten in the land of Egypt; and the famine will deplete the land. So the plenty will not be known in the land because of the famine following, for it will be very severe.* **And the dream was repeated to Pharaoh twice because the thing is established by God, and God will shortly bring it to pass.** *Now therefore, let Pharaoh select a discerning and wise man, and set him over the land of Egypt. Let Pharaoh do this, and let him appoint officers over the land, to collect one-fifth of the produce of the land of Egypt in the seven plentiful years. And let them gather all the food of those good years that are coming, and store up grain under the authority of Pharaoh, and let them keep food in the cities. Then that food shall be as a reserve for the land for the seven years of famine which shall be in the land of Egypt, that the land may not perish during the famine.'" Genesis 41:8-36 (emphasis mine)*

I never cease to be amazed when I read this passage at the powerful way in which God used Joseph. It was truly a victory for Joseph to be brought out of prison to interpret a dream for Pharaoh, thus putting an end to his imprisonment and resulting in a national promotion. In one day, Joseph went from the jailhouse to the palace all because he knew how to hear the voice of God in dreams. That would be like you receiving a job offer at the White House because you were summoned by the President of the United States to interpret his dream for him. May we get to that level of skill and wisdom in hearing the voice of God!

Joseph cooperated very eloquently with God as He gave God all the glory before Pharaoh and as he provided the accurate interpretation. Then to put the frosting on the cake, Joseph went a step beyond the interpretation and gave Pharaoh God's wisdom in applying the interpretation. He spoke the strategy of what to do with the information God gave him to prevent the famine. This is a great example of someone operating in the gift of word of wisdom, which gives us God's strategy, wisdom and direction for specific future events.

So what does this mean for you? Quit scaring Aunt Sue by telling her that you had a dream in which she got hit by a bus. You are scaring her and will probably be responsible for any fears that she develops as a result of your dream. The fact that you dreamt about her doesn't mean that the dream was about her.

People have often told me that they dreamed something and then it happened exactly as they saw it in their dreams. I have a theory about why that happens. I believe that God knows what level we are at in understanding His voice in dreams. Being that He really wants to communicate with us, He will at times speak to us on our level. In other words, He may give us literal dreams because that's all we understand. Let me clarify the misconception that these literal dreams are the good ones.

Actually, I find that these are the entry-level dreams. Once we start maturing in hearing God's voice in dreams, our dreams start becoming more complex. God is always interested in our growth and does not want us to stay infants. Let's not act like infants when God begins to remove the bottle of milk from our mouths to give us more solid food. Don't start complaining when your dreams transition from literal to more complex. Take this as a sign that you are growing in understanding the language of the Holy Spirit in dreams and that you are going to a higher level.

So now, let's go back to that example dream with Aunt Sue being hit by a bus. We need to fight off all temptation to look at this dream literally. As you're learning to interpret your dreams, here is a question you should always ask yourself. "If that is not really (the person or subject in the dream), then who or what could it be?" So, in this case, if that is not Aunt Sue, then what could it be? So looking at our example dream, I could tell you now that Aunt Sally is a symbol of something – she represents something in your life. Whatever she represents in your life is in danger of being hurt.

This is a skill that you could begin to develop and grow in. Begin to ask God to help you develop your understanding of symbols and how to interpret them. He will be faithful to give you what you need. Remember, if anyone wants you to understand the voice of God in dreams, it is God Himself. We'll get into symbolism suggestions a little further in this chapter.

Literal dreams are more prophetic than you know!

Literal dreams are the exception and not the rule. We have all had dreams that were literal in nature and came to pass shortly afterward. God is God and He can and will show us scenes that will occur in the future. But, could there be more to it that we've been missing? Let's not approach literal dreams on a superficial, shallow level. I believe that there is more than what meets the eye.

So, for example, let's say you dreamed that your coworker Bruno got a divorce, only to find out in real life that he is moving towards his divorce. God showed what would happen ahead of time, but for what purpose? Was it to warn Bruno? To pray for him? To witness the downfall of his marriage completely helpless from the sidelines?

Let me first say that I believe God always wants us to have a response of prayer. In this case, when you find out that Bruno is really getting a divorce, you start to pray for him and his marriage. Regardless of the outcome, whether the divorce goes through or not, we can do the right thing by at least praying.

Now, let's get your view off the literal event that took place. Rather than just saying that God showed you a future event, let's take another spin on this "revelation". We would have to question God's reason for showing you what was going to happen. Remember, God wants to use you to be a blessing in Bruno's life by praying for him, but He also wants to continually speak to *you* about *your* life. So I would advise the dreamer to look into his own life to see if there is a prophetic message for him.

1 – Would there be a connection with your own marriage? Is your marriage also in trouble? Could this dream be a warning that something is wrong in your own marriage?

2 – Let's say that when I ask the dreamer how he would describe Bruno, he says he's "not committed." Could that be symbolic for what's going on in your life? Would there be a relationship that you're not committed to that is in danger? Maybe a relationship with a friend, a family member, your church, etc.? I would instruct the dreamer to search his life to see if there is a fit for this symbolic warning.

So as you see, many times we take literal dreams all too literal when God may be trying to convey a deeper message to us. Even when the event takes place in the natural, God may be re-speaking the message to us. So in this example, the divorce went through and through the actual act, God is re-speaking the warning to your life. Am I saying that God caused their divorce? No, absolutely not! I'm just saying that God knows what will occur in the future and will use that knowledge for His purposes.

When you have a dream that your brother tripped and fell only to find out later that he actually did, don't leave it as a surface revelation. Go down deeper and pray to see if whatever your brother represents in your life is in danger of falling and getting hurt. By taking this approach to literal dreams, we begin to realize that God will even use life events as prophetic messages for our lives.

God is not interested in having believers have knowledge of the future only so that they could look super spiritual. "You see what took place in John Doe's life? God showed me that in a dream before it happened." Those arrogant statements should not come from Anointed Detectives. We are always looking to hear the voice of God for our own lives. Whenever God does use us as a prophetic voice for someone else, it is always for God's glory.

#3 – Not all dreams are God-given.

Please do me a favor and make sure that you re-read the title right above this sentence right next to #3. It amazes me while teaching the Hearing the Voice of God class how many times I would say that not all dreams were God-given dreams, someone would later in the class say, "So, are you saying that you believe that all dreams are from God?" Their lack of hearing me greatly frustrated me. Therefore, before you ask the same question, let me make it clear that I do not believe that all dreams are from God. As a matter of fact the Bible supports this point in the following verse:

> *"For a dream comes through much activity, and a fool's voice is known by his many words." Ecclesiastes 5:3 (emphasis mine)*

Much Activity

We need to understand that every living human being dreams. God never designed our brains to shut off after we go to sleep. Our brains continue to be active even after we have called it a night. So from the above Scripture, we can see that dreams can be the result of having much of certain activities that take place in our day. It is not uncommon to dream of hockey if you spent your day watching a hockey game.

What I've come to learn, however, is that once we make Jesus the Lord of our nights as He is the Lord of our days, God will begin to use those activities that we were involved in that day to speak to us a spiritual message.

Medication

We live in a time of much sickness and disease. There are medications today for just about any illness that exists. Unfortunately, some of these medications have side effects that range from rashes to dry mouth. One side effect that I have heard people complain of is crazy dreams. Whenever these individuals are under the influence of certain medications, they report that their dreams are wild and at times terrifying.

I would highly recommend anyone who is in this category to seek out some trusted spiritual friends from your church and have them pray over you. Have them declare the promise over you that God has provided out of Psalms 127.

> *"It is vain for you to rise up early, to sit up late, to eat the bread of sorrows; **for so He gives His beloved sleep**." Psalms 127:2 (emphasis mine)*

Demonic Attacks

While our bodies may need at least eight hours of rest daily, we have an enemy who does not rest. He is constantly looking for ways to come against us and to introduce his plan to steal, kill and destroy our lives. One of the ways that he does this is by tormenting us with nightmares.

Now, a nightmare is very different from a God-given dream. The reason why I am even comparing them is because some God-given dreams are so vivid in nature that when the person wakes up their emotions are wrapped up into the dream. These dreams can be so vivid that we may easily mistake them for a nightmare.

I once worked with a gentleman who was a believer. He and his wife were the worship leaders at their local church. After talking with him about dreams, he shared with me that he never remembered any of his dreams, let alone had any God-given dreams. I prayed with him a prayer of impartation to hear the voice of God in dreams. The next day as he walked into work, I asked him if he had a dream. Immediately a look of fear came across his face. "What's the matter?" I asked curiously.

"Well, thanks to your prayer, I didn't have a dream. I had a nightmare," he said quite annoyed.

"A nightmare? Are you sure it was a nightmare?"

"Yes, it was a nightmare. It was so terrible that I don't want to remember it.

"Well," I paused to select the right words, "why don't you tell me your nightmare so that I can understand you better?"

"Okay. Well, I dreamed that my wife and I were lying down on our bed. As I looked over to my wife, I saw that she was in tremendous pain. It looked as if she were travailing and bringing forth a baby. It was clear that she was very tormented with pain and I was heartbroken to see her like that. I felt helpless. All I could do was idly observe. Suddenly, she opened her mouth and fruit began to come out of her mouth. One by one, different kinds of fruit began to emerge. That's when I woke up. It was so vivid that when I woke up my heart was pounding."

No matter how much I tried to resist, I couldn't help but smile as my friend relayed his dream to me. "Why are you smiling?" he asked me.

"You didn't have a nightmare," I responded.

"I didn't?" he replied, almost robotically.

"No. You think it was a nightmare because of how vivid the dream was. It was only vivid because God was talking loudly to you about the stage that you are in with your ministry. The dream was symbolic. I believe that God was showing you that while you and your wife are in a place of rest, there is some travailing that will begin to take place as you birth what God has in store for you. The dream is also to assure you not to be concerned with the travailing but to know that it will bear fruit in the end."

With the look on my friend's face, I could tell that he was now a believer in hearing the voice of God in dreams. A few months later, he shared with me how the travailing had begun in their ministry and what he thought it would mean for their future. I am confident that they will walk into the fullness of what God has for them.

A nightmare can be identified because nightmares have an element of fear and torment in them. I believe that nightmares are more than just a scary scene in a dream; I believe they are actually a spirit of fear coming against you in the night season. That demonic spirit cloaks itself within a nightmare in order to present itself to the dreamer. Remember, God is not interested in scaring you to the point that you cannot function normally after that. Any dream that leaves you tormented or unable to function due to fear is a nightmare.

Nightmares also include dreams that are graphically sexual for the purpose of enticing one to open the door to a spirit of lust. If these types of nightmares are entertained, the sleeper will open a door to these perverted spirits and will walk in a higher level of lust and perversion. Only Jesus Christ can deliver the person from these oppressive spirits and set them truly free.

Nightmares don't have to go that far in extremity. They could just be regular dreams that cause torment. I have conversed with many Christians that suffer from nightmares on an almost nightly basis. These are Christians who love the Lord, but don't understand why God hasn't helped them stop the nightmares from occurring. After being exposed to this dilemma several times and asking many questions, I have found some repetitive problems that have allowed these nightmares to continue in the lives of believers. Remember that Satan cannot continue to come attack you with nightmares unless he has a reason to do so. Let's look at some of those reasons.

1 – Unconfessed sin. Sin is an open door to the enemy to come into your life and wreak havoc. The Bible warns us not to open the door to the devil.

> *"In your anger do not sin": Do not let the sun go down while you are still angry, and do not give the devil a foothold. He who has been stealing must steal no longer, but must work, doing something useful with his own hands, that he may have something to share with those in need." Ephesians 4:26-28*

I would describe a foothold as leaving a door open just enough so that someone can maneuver their way in. We cannot continue to live our lives the way that we used to before we walked with the Lord. To do so is to give the devil a foothold in our lives and to welcome him to come against us.

2 – Involvement in the occult. No doubt about it, if you are involved somehow in the occult, you have opened a big door to Satan

to come into your life and wreak havoc. This is not meant to be an extensive list, but here are some examples of occult activity that will open the door to the enemy:

> ~ Going to a psychic, fortune-teller, tarot card reader or medium to tell you your fortune. This involves any other person who is speaking to you about your life outside of the realm of the Holy Spirit.

> ~ Reading your horoscopes or any literature that will foretell your future.

> ~ Possessing literature regarding the occult and how to develop and get involved in it.

> ~ Possessing and/or playing games such as the Ouija Board or role-playing fantasy games such as Dungeons and Dragons.

> ~ Having charms, amulets or crystals that are supposed to bring you luck.

> ~ Possessing anything that may have demonic attachments to it. Be cautious as to what items you bring into your house. Demons may attach themselves to items and when they are brought into a home, the demons are given full reign to operate and bring oppression.

I once was called to the home of a friend who was having bad experiences in his home. As we prayed through the house, I was asking God to reveal what was the cause of the demonic oppression in the home. Suddenly, my eyes were drawn to two large ceramic lions that sat on either side of the fireplace. I had a strange eerie feeling as I observed them. Their features were grotesque, and I couldn't imagine what made my friend put those ugly statues by his fireplace. He later explained that they were a bargain at a garage sale. (Be careful what you pick up at garage sales!) After I shared that revelation with my friend, he took them outside and destroyed the ceramic lions. He later confirmed that the oppressive atmosphere of the house was cleared up.

~ Horror movies. Please do not be deceived. Horror movies are movies that promote fear. It is possible to not be able to sleep for many days after watching one of these movies. I don't allow myself the opportunity to view these types of movies. They present the viewer with horrifying plots, terrible situations and demonic characters that only open the door further to the spirit of fear. It goes against the things that the Bible tells us that we should meditate on. "Finally, brothers, whatever is true, whatever is noble, whatever is right, whatever is pure, whatever is lovely, whatever is admirable – if anything is excellent or praiseworthy – think about such things." Philippians 4:8

~ Any other item (movie, book, article, game, involvement in some activity) that promotes devil worship and/or idolatry and encourages the person to move further away from God.

3 – Ignorance. One of the major reasons why the enemy is so successful in continuing to bombard us with nightmares is because we are ignorant of the promises of God. If believers knew who they were in Christ and believed the promises of God, they would not allow the enemy to attack them with nightmares. Remember that Psalms 127:2 says that He gives His beloved sleep. That is a promise from God that you could take seriously.

Nightmares should be treated on the same level as a thief breaking into your house to steal. Does a thief have the right to come into your house and steal from you anytime he desires? No, absolutely not! Neither does the enemy have the right to come and torment us with a nightmare. If they are occurring in our lives, then it is a clear sign that we must pray and ask the Lord to reveal what doors we have opened to the devil so that we could close them once and for all.

We must be on our guard to thwart the devil's attack on our lives through nightmares. This doesn't mean that we're to try to stay up all night to prevent him from bringing a nightmare. We are to use our

God-given authority, and we are to run the devil out of our homes and lives.

Nightmares & Children

I would also like to address the topic of children having night-mares. The enemy of our souls loves to present his plan for our lives at an early age. He loves to go after our children. If he can get them to receive a spirit of fear from him at an early age, he has a head start.

My oldest daughter Alyssa began to have regular nightmares that were bothersome. I was continually becoming frustrated at my lack of being able to get these to stop. I would pray over my house and search to see if I had brought something into my house that shouldn't have been there. No matter how much I prayed and searched the house, she would continue to have nightmares. One day during prayer, I discerned that the enemy was trying to traumatize my daughter with those nightmares. It angered me so much that I asked the Holy Spirit to give me wisdom on how to pray against the devil's plan. Immediately, I was inspired to pray that my daughter Alyssa would develop a strong dreamer's anointing for God's glory. Just as Satan tried to come against her in her dreams, I prayed that God would use her dreams to communicate to her and that she would be a modern-day Daniel in the Body of Christ.

A few days after starting to pray for my daughter the way the Holy Spirit prompted me, the attacks against her stopped. Her dreams started becoming more prophetic in nature. Alyssa has been taken to heaven 3 times in dreams and has seen the Lord as well.

What I have found is that God will turn what Satan has meant for evil and will use it for good. Praise God! Satan wanted to introduce fear to my daughter through nightmares, but God has switched it around, and my daughter is now operating in a powerful seer's anointing and is hearing from God in her dreams.

If your son or daughter is suffering from nightmares, remember to go through your house and take spiritual inventory to see if you have opened the door to the enemy. If you haven't, however, under-stand that Satan may be trying to make his mark on their lives. You must anoint your children and pray over their night seasons that God would use it for His glory. We usually only teach our children about how to serve the Lord while we are awake. We have neglected to also instruct our children that God desires to communicate to them while they are asleep. We must prepare them at young ages to be alert to His voice while they are resting on their beds. To train them at an early age is to prepare them for a life of seeking after the Lord.

I want to share with you an example of one of the beautiful things that God did for my daughter Alyssa shortly after her nightmares stopped and she began to flow in a stronger prophetic anointing in her dreams. I love to call this story the "Pie Story."

Alyssa was in the second grade and her teacher had a system in place to reward students who were good listeners. Every time a student made a right decision, the teacher would give them a point. For every ten points the student would accumulate, their names were put on a chart in the classroom and they would receive a small prize. As they accumulated ten more points, they would go higher on the prize chart. So for ten points, they may have received a pencil or a pen. At twenty points, they may have received a small notebook. The highest designation was when they received 60 points. At this level, their names would be placed on a picture of a pie at the top of the chart. The prize for reaching the pie was that the student could pick two friends to join them for lunch in the classroom as opposed to eating in the cafeteria. From the beginning of the school year, Alyssa kept mentioning to me that she really wanted to reach the pie.

One day, as Alyssa got home from school, I noticed that she looked really sad.

"What's wrong Alyssa?" I asked concerned.

"Dad, remember when I told you that I wanted to reach the pie? Well, I'm only five good choices away from getting there," she replied.

"Honey, congratulations. That's great! So, why are you so sad?"

"Well, I'm only five points away, and I really want to reach the pie, but I can't."

"Yes, you can. Honey, just keep making good decisions, and your teacher will give you the points that you need."

"I do keep making good decisions, but my teacher doesn't give me the points. She gives them to other students. I don't know what else to do."

"There is only one thing that we can do. We can ask the Lord to help us. He knows the desire of your heart, and He answers prayer. So let's pray and ask Jesus to help us." I noticed that a look of relief came across her face as I took her hands in mine. "Jesus," I prayed out loud, " Alyssa really wants to reach the pie. You see what a great job she's doing at school. Your word tells us that You give us the desires of our heart. Please help Alyssa make the right decisions so that she can reach that pie. In Jesus name we pray, Amen." With that simple prayer, the conversation was over.

A few days later, Alyssa jumped out of the school bus ecstatic. "Dad, dad," she shouted loudly, "I reached the pie. I get to pick two friends, and on Friday we'll eat lunch in the classroom and not in the cafeteria. Can you believe it?"

"Of course I can believe it. We prayed, didn't we? Now being that we prayed, let's stop and thank the Lord for His help." As we grabbed hands and prayed, I could see that my daughter was so excited she almost shouted her "Amen". The Friday of her lunch came and went as she continued her school year.

A few days later, Alyssa approached me one morning and said, "Dad, I had a very interesting dream last night."

"Yeah? Well, why don't you tell me."

"Okay," she said inhaling and exhaling deeply. "Well, I was in the kitchen getting ready to eat some food when suddenly I heard a trumpet blast in the living room. I walked over to the living room and saw that there was a cloud floating close to the ceiling of the living room. Suddenly, something lifted me up to where the cloud was. As I reached the top of the cloud, I saw Jesus and He was surrounded by many angels wearing white robes. Jesus suddenly told me, 'Alyssa, I have come to tell you, congratulations on reaching the pie.'"

As she told me those words, tears began to fill my eyes as I realized that my Jesus was making Himself known personally to my daughter. Here the Lord was letting Alyssa know that He heard her prayer and had responded. My heart's desire has always been that my daughters would know the Lord personally at an early age. How awesome!

As I write this book, my youngest daughter Leilani is now step-ping into her dreamer's anointing. I am regularly amazed at the depth of revelation that God releases to her in her dreams. I am excited for their futures knowing that they will always hunger for the things of God.

I included that story to encourage you to pray for your children's dream lives and to instruct them on how God uses dreams for His purposes. You will be amazed at how God will communicate with your children through their dreams. It's never too late to start. Let's prepare the next generations to walk in the full prophetic mantle that God has for them.

#4 – The more you pay attention to dreams, the more God-given dreams you will have.

Not paying attention to our dreams is like closing the valve that stops water from flowing. I've heard believers say that they don't have dreams. Upon further examination, it is easy to see that it's usually because they have ignored their dreams for years. As a result they will go through life unaware of the powerful vehicle that they have available to hear God's voice.

Christians that are dull in hearing from God didn't end up in that condition overnight. It has taken a process of months and maybe even years of ignoring and turning a deaf ear. In order to begin the flow of dreams in their lives, they would have to go back and begin to open the "valve" to allow the revelation to start flowing once again. By paying attention to your dreams, you are slowly building up your ability to hear from God in them.

First, by paying attention to your dreams, you are becoming intentional. Once God knows that you are paying attention to your dreams, He has more to work with in us and will begin to inspire more dreams from His realm.

Second, the flow increases. Now the trickle of dreams turns into a heavy flow of constant communication. Can you imagine that? A constant flow of communication in dreams? Now we don't only hear God while we're awake, but we could go to sleep and continue hearing His voice. How cool is that? That is what I call a win / win situation.

Some people dream dreams that are more out of the natural realm as opposed to God-given dreams. These people will also benefit from heeding the advice #4. If they would pay attention and ask for God-given dreams, they will begin to have more of them, which will benefit their lives. You have to dream anyway. Why not give God your night season so that He can use your dreams to talk to you? Makes perfect sense to me. I hope you'll agree.

#5 – You don't need someone with a "gift of dream interpretation."

I hear this almost everywhere I go. In every church, at least one person will make the claim that they have the "gift of dream interpretation." People in the church seek them out and look for this "expert" to tell them what their dreams mean.

There is no "gift of dream interpretation" just like there is no "gift of dreams." It is not one of the gifts of the Holy Spirit listed in 1 Corinthians 12. Just as we have all been designed by God to dream in the night season, we can all develop our own ability to interpret our dreams. When we get accustomed to running to a certain individual to interpret our dreams, we are giving him/her a place of control and maybe even manipulation in our lives. God wants you to develop your own skill to interpret dreams.

There is nothing wrong with seeking the help of someone more seasoned than you. The main focus, however, has to be on you learning for yourself as opposed to giving this person the role of your personal dream interpreter.

"Dreams" is a topic that is very close to my heart. I have learned from the person who mentored me in dreams, Pastor Benny Thomas, not to be quick to become a personal dream interpreter for anyone.

As I developed in my understanding of dreams and interpretation, I have had many people run to me and repeatedly asked me to interpret dreams for them. Whatever interpretation I would give them would be set in stone for them, due to the fact that I was developing quite a reputation as an accurate dream interpreter.

After awhile, however, I started feeling the effects of burnout. I got tired of trying to leave church quickly only to be approached by many people to help them with dreams. I got tired of having a full email box of people asking for my help with their dreams. I also got very tired of people not considering my family as they would aggressively interrupt us at any moment with a dream needing interpretation and would not take no for an answer. This resulted in many cases when my family would be out waiting for me in the car (at times for almost up to an hour) while I interpreted a dream for someone. Then, I started really understanding what my mentor was warning me about from the beginning. In my zeal to grow and develop in the skill of dream interpretation, I had unknowingly made myself the official interpreter for those around me.

In order to correct this, I quickly changed my approach. Rather than allow people to interrupt me and ask for help with a dream, I started teaching a class on dreams and would politely tell the person that if they wanted help with their dreams, they would have to commit to taking a class to learn more about dreams. Also, rather than give everyone a solidified interpretation, I began to work with each person to help them interpret their dream. I would ask them questions to assist them in arriving at their conclusions, which would develop their dream interpretation skills. This new approach did two good things for me. First, this caused the lazy folks to avoid me because they wanted me to do all of the work. Secondly, it resulted in those truly interested in learning how to develop their own skill of interpretation to learn and to grow.

You have what it takes to develop your skill of dream interpretation. Take to heart Joseph's words, "***It is not in me; God will give Pharaoh an answer of peace.***" Interpretations belong to God. If we are truly interested, He will teach us His ways.

#6 – Dream tenses.

I find it very helpful to know which tense dreams usually address-past, present or future. I have found that the majority of dreams will deal with what you are presently walking through, or what you're about to step into. God is always looking to help us find our way as we are being led by His Spirit.

When you are looking to interpret a dream, approach it with the slant that the dream is dealing with present and future events. It's not to say that God can't speak to us about the past in our dreams; He can and He most likely will. However, God always wants for us to learn from our mistakes and from our pasts and move forward. We are to always look ahead as God leads us into our destinies. Likewise, I have found that dreams are a powerful vehicle to hear from God for what is occurring now and for what is about to unfold.

#7 – Types of dreams.

You may be wondering what kind of dreams God could send your way. There are various types. Let's look at these.

Spiritual Dreams

God will use these dreams to talk to you about your spiritual life. He will regularly address your relationship with Him and will reveal to you what He is requiring of you to bring it to a higher level.

I recently held a Dream Interpretation Night at the café in my local church. One visitor shared with me a recurring dream she had been having in which her son was repeatedly being violated sexually by a perpetrator. It caused her much anxiety and she constantly interviewed her son (in real life) to make sure that this wasn't really happening. She explained to me that she had been having this dream for years. After asking her son, who is now close to being an adult, he continued to assure her that nothing of the like had occurred, to her relief.

"Well," I said to her, "dreams usually deal with present or future events. Being that this was not literal, and nothing of the sort has happened to your son, it is obviously symbolic. Your son represents something in your life that is in danger of being violated. We have to find out what it is. Is there an area of your life that you feel is in danger?"

"No," she replied after taking some time to ponder carefully.

"Now, we are trying to find out what your son represents. When we get this, we will unlock the interpretation. Let's look at your son symbolically. He is something that you have brought forth from your own life. Is there anything that you have brought forth that is in danger of being violated?"

"I'm not sure," she bluntly responded.

"Okay, so when you have this recurring dream, do you notice a pattern of something going wrong in your life?" As I asked the question, I could see a smile coming across her face.

"Yes. I have backslidden several times from my walk with God. I love the Lord, and I know I have a calling on my life, but for some reason, sometimes I notice that I start getting spiritually cold. It's usually around that time when I notice I have the recurring dream with my son."

"Bingo!" I shouted. "We have the interpretation. Just as you have brought your son forth from your own life and you have nourished and nurtured him into the young man he is today, God is showing you that your walk with the Lord must also be nourished and nurtured. Just as how you would protect your child in the natural from a sexual perpetrator, you must also protect your walk with the Lord from the devil who is out to destroy your inheritance in God. You were taking it literal and were fearful for your son. At the same time, however, you were not protecting your walk with the Lord, and God was warning you that your walk with Him was unprotected and vulnerable." As I shared the interpretation of the dream, the presence of the Holy Spirit was strong upon us both. We could tell that the interpretation was sure. God loved her so much that he warned her to keep her spiritual walk protected.

As you hear from God in dreams, expect Him to address your spiritual life, as He most certainly will.

Teaching Dreams

Dreams are also a vehicle in which God will provide instruction to you. Your learning doesn't have to end when you go to sleep. The citizens of the Kingdom of Heaven may continue their download of knowledge and wisdom even as we sleep. God may teach you more about the Scriptures or more about Himself. When we are in the School of the Holy Spirit, the courses are limitless.

Creativity Dreams

Creative and non-creative people beware. God will download creativity to you as you allow Him to communicate to you in dreams. That translates into musicians getting songs in their dreams. Artists will receive ideas for paintings in their dreams. God can provide ideas for inventions in dreams. Again, the options are limitless.

I once went to the home of an older lady from our church that was ill. I went with a group of young adults to go and encourage her. As she was sharing with us, I couldn't help but notice the beautiful chandelier that was hanging in her living room. When she saw me looking up at it, she said, "Oh, let me tell you the story of that chandelier. I have always wanted one and being that I couldn't afford to purchase one, I asked God to show me how to make one. After making my request of the Lord, I had a dream in which a guy walked into my room with all of the materials to make the chandelier. Step by step he assembled it carefully enough so that I could see what he was doing until the project was complete. When I woke up, I absolutely knew how to make the chandelier. I went to the store and purchased all of the materials, and there you have it. The rest is history." We were in awe at how God could download such information in a dream. The evidence, however, hung right before my very eyes – a beautifully elegant chandelier.

If you need creativity, ask God for it. After all, He is the true Creator of the arts. Just take a look at the world that He has fashioned for us. Father God is truly the Master Artist.

Warning Dreams

One of the perks of serving the one true living God is that He will warn us ahead of time of anything that may threaten our safety. He doesn't warn us to scare or frighten us, but to move us into prayer to change the course of things. Or, for those things that are set to occur, to minimize the damage.

If God gives you a warning in a dream, don't be frightened or despair. Look at it as a message of love from a Father who protects His children.

Other Kinds of Dreams

We can never say that we know everything that God can and will do. To make such a statement would expose arrogance and deception. As His children, just when we think we have God all figured out, He will then reveal another aspect of Himself that we didn't know before. We are always learning more about Him.

On that note, God may use dreams to speak to you about anything. I'm sure that He can show you where the lost item you've been looking for is. I'm sure that He can reveal to you the real problem as to why your children are being rebellious. The beauty of it is that God does all the talking He wants as we do the listening. My prayer to the Lord is that He will speak to me about every area of my life, even the areas that are difficult for me to have Him address. We need to be very open before Him.

How Dreams Work

Okay, so let's look at how God-given dreams work in our lives. Through dreams God can speak to us about any and every area of our lives. He will talk to you about your friendships, your school, your career, your children, your finances, your health, your ministry, your hindrances, etc. God will talk to you about all areas so that you can grow in Him.

rmula to hear from God in dreams.

 you a dream.

rate with God to arrive at the interpretation.

! You could start hearing the voice of God in no time
. Let's go over the each part of the formula.

#1 – God gives you a dream.

Throughout the Bible, we read that dreams were one of the major ways that God spoke to His people. Through a dream God revealed Joseph's future position of authority. Through a dream God imparted wisdom to King Solomon. Through a dream, Joseph was warned of the danger that threatened baby Jesus' life. As a result, His life was spared because Joseph was able to take baby Jesus out of the country. These are all examples of how God spoke to His children through dreams.

God continues to use dreams as a way to communicate His will to us today. In order to hear from God in dreams, we need to dream dreams.

A – Ask God to speak to you in dreams. That may be the main reason why you're not dreaming. Start off by praying a prayer of faith. Repent for any areas of doubt and unbelief and commit to God your night seasons.

B – Put a note pad and a pen by your bedside. This is an act of faith! Let God know that you mean business. With that act alone, you are showing God that if He speaks to you in dreams, you will respond by writing them out. This is a prophetic act that speaks loudly.

Journaling is an important part of developing your skill to hear from God in dreams. I've heard the complaint about not having enough time in the day to journal. You could try something else such as a tape recorder or some other method to record your dream. Whatever system you choose, you must be committed to continue using it on a daily basis.

C – When waking up from a dream, try to recall your dream. This is the part of the dreaming process that will make or break our success. The Bible says in Job 20:8, *"He will fly away like a dream, and not be found; yes, he will be chased away like a vision of the night."* This verse shows accurately what happens with dreams once we've had them. They easily fly away from us. Therefore, it is so important to grab a firm hold on these dreams and write them out in our journals before we forget them.

The main reason why dreams fly away is because we wake up from our sleep and go about our day without trying to recall the dream. Out of habit, we will usually jump out of bed and go about our morning routines. Therefore, here is what I would recommend you do before getting up. As you lie in bed, ask yourself, "Did I have a dream last night?" Look for pieces to come floating to your mind so that you could reconstruct the whole dream again. Get into the habit of doing this to help you retain your God-given dreams.

D – Journal the dream. You will not be able to remember all of your dreams by memory. You'll need to actually sit down and write them out. I suggest that you get a notebook only for your dreams. Call it your "Dream Journal". My daughters have observed me for years writing in my dream journal, and one Christmas they asked me for Dream Journals as presents. I was very excited to see that I was promoting a prophetic-dream excitement in my home.

When writing your dream, make sure to number each page in your journal and include the date. By writing down the dates, you can easily look back to see what time in your life God was speaking to you about a particular subject. For matters that we'll discuss later in this book, knowing the dates of your dreams comes in handy. I would also recommend using one page per dream. I have seen journals where many dreams are crammed onto one page. You need room to write down your thoughts and possible interpretations. Limit the pages to one dream per page.

Now that you are receiving God-given dreams and are doing your part to recall them and journal them, we'll need to know how to interpret the dream so that we can gain understanding of its message.

#2 – You cooperate with God to arrive at the interpretation.

I love the statement Joseph made in the presence of Pharaoh when he said, "*It is not in me; God will give Pharaoh an answer of peace.*" *(Genesis 41)* Now that we're hearing from God, we need to cooperate with Him to receive the interpretations. This is the part that causes many people to get nervous. If that's you, shake yourself from all of that anxiety and find refuge in the statement that Joseph made. Interpretations belong to God and He will give an answer of peace.

Before we get into interpretation techniques, let's look at an important component to this process.

Get and stay in the Spirit.

The best way to stay in tune with the voice of God is to stay in the Spirit. The Apostle John described this point well in the book of Revelation.

> "*After these things I looked, and behold, a door standing open in heaven. And the first voice which I heard was like a trumpet speaking with me, saying, 'Come up here, and I will show you things which must take place after this.'* **Immediately I was in the Spirit***; and behold, a throne set in heaven, and One sat on the throne. And He who sat there was like a jasper and a sardius stone in appearance; and there was a rainbow around the throne, in appearance like an emerald.*" *Revelation 4:1-3 (emphasis mine)*

When John received this revelation, he was on the island of Patmos. In an instant, he was in the Spirit and stood in heaven observing a beautiful scene. He was able to receive the message of end-time prophecy while he was in the Spirit. I define being in the Spirit as living in a state of being constantly in tune with the voice of God. It is to live in such a close intimacy with the Father that you are obedient to Him and His word.

The Bible tells us the results of what living in the Spirit means.

> "*I say then: Walk in the Spirit and you shall not fulfill the lust of the flesh*" *Galatians 5:16*

Now, in a previous chapter, I mentioned about how God created us as a spirit with a soul that lives in a body. We are a triune being! It is in our spirits where the Holy Spirit comes to take residence. That is why the Bible says in 1 Corinthians 6:19, "Or did you not know that your body is a temple of the Holy Spirit who is in you, whom you have from God and you are not your own?" Our bodies carry our spirit man within, and our spirits serve as the dwelling place of the Holy Spirit. Therefore, He lives within us.

As believers, we could walk our Christian walk in the flesh or in the Spirit. The choice is ours. If you wanted to walk in the flesh, God would not force you to change your mind. He's given you free will to do so. Now, the problem with walking in the flesh is that as a result, we will fulfill every lust that is raging within the flesh.

If we choose to walk in the Spirit, as a result, we don't fulfill the lusts of the flesh. Not only are we not fulfilling the lust of the flesh, but now it is easier for us to be led by God and to hear His voice. There is a sensitivity to the voice of God that comes as a result of being in the Spirit.

Now, being in the Spirit is not something that has to be done for a short while and then you get out of the Spirit. We can live our entire Christian lives in the Spirit, being led by God, not giving place to the lusts of our flesh and enjoying an intimacy with God the Father.

Here's how you can get into the Spirit and stay there:

~ Live a life of prayer. Prayer is what keeps you face to face with the Father.

~ Study the Scriptures to stay close the Father's heart.

~ Pray in the Holy Ghost daily. "But you, beloved, building yourself up on your most holy faith, praying in the Holy Spirit." Jude 1:20 While you're spending time in prayer, make sure to spend time praying in tongues. As you do that, you eventually come to a place where you feel a difference in the realm around you. You'll know it when you are in the Spirit; it'll be obvious to you.

I was once pressing in to God praying for an answer that I desperately needed. I prayed and prayed when suddenly I heard the
Holy Spirit tell me, "Now pray in your prayer language." I then started
praying in tongues. On and on I went praying in my heavenly language. About ninety minutes later, I heard the Holy Spirit say, "You
are now in the Spirit." I felt it! I knew that something had taken place
because I felt as if I was under an open heaven. It was truly amazing. I continued to pray and press in until the Lord rewarded me with
the answer that I was waiting for.

By being in the Spirit, it is much easier for us to hear the voice of
God and receive interpretations for our dreams. How difficult it is for
those who are in the flesh to hear God clearly. We could get so
frustrated and wonder why God isn't talking clearly to us. Part of the
problem may be that you may be walking in the flesh, which makes it
more difficult for us to hear God. I'm not saying this to condemn
anyone. There is hope in Jesus! If you find yourself walking in the
flesh, go immediately into your prayer closet and do not come out
until you are in the Spirit, until you've broken through to the realm of
the Spirit. Then, continue to pray daily and keep yourself in that
realm. God's voice will become more natural to you and easier to
discern as a result. This will help you receive interpretations to your
dreams easier.

Technique 1 — Read the dream as a whole and see if it fits any area of your life.

This technique works for dreams that are very short and quick. If
it is a short enough dream, you may be able to see if what you saw in
the dream fits your life. If it does, once God confirms it to you, you
would have yourself an interpretation.

Let me give you an example. I once had a very short dream
where I walked into a college and walked up to a registration table.
The lady asked me for my name and I gave it to her. As she looked
at all the files on her desk, she pulled my file, opened and gave me a
piece of paper that was inside the file. The paper read, "Paid in full."
The dream ended. Well, while the dream didn't literally take place in
that I never walked up to a lady at a college and had her give me a
sheet of paper saying "Paid in full", the message did fit my life.

At the time, I was working full-time and was studying part-time at a local college. I had been hired into a position that required a college degree, which I didn't possess. I was hired with the stipulation that I would go back to college to work on completing my degree. I was paying from my own salary to go to school while I was supporting my family. My wife was a stay-at-home mom, and therefore, every cent that went towards my college degree was money that went out of my family's pocket. I was getting ready to start a new semester and was not sure if I would be able to afford it. Getting frustrated at the rising cost of going to school, I took my complaint to the Lord. Shortly afterward, I had the above-mentioned dream.

Shortly after having that God-given dream, I received a note in the mail informing me that I had won a scholarship to continue my studies. Unbeknownst to me, one of my professors had submitted my name as a candidate for this highly competitive scholarship. After having been awarded the scholarship, I was able to complete my degree at no further cost to me. Praise God! Through that brief dream, God was informing me that He was going to supply my needs so that I could finish my studies.

If your dream is a short one, try this technique. If this doesn't fit, we'll have to try some other techniques.

Longer Dreams: Divide the dream into sections, then apply technique #1.

I find that shorter dreams are usually the exception. Dreams tend to be longer than just one scene. I've written many dreams into my journal that had multiple scenes. Here's how you handle the longer dreams while applying technique #1.

As you write a dream down in your journal, skip a line between scenes. Separate each scene of the dream and write them as different paragraphs. Journaling the dreams correctly in the beginning saves you from having to go back and do the work later.

I assign numbers to each scene. So when I'm writing down one of my dreams, I put a (#1) in the margin as I write out that scene of the dream. When I go on to the next scene, I skip a line and then write (#2) in the margin and continue to journal. That way, all of my lengthier dreams are already divided into sections for interpretation.

It's almost like what you did in technique number one. Now that the dream is broken down into segments, you are going to look at each segment to see if it fits some area of your life, just like I did in the above dream example. If this doesn't fit, we'll have to try the other techniques.

Technique #2 – Try to interpret the symbols.

Remember, a dream is like a symbolic movie that has a message for your life. Once the dream is divided into sections, take the first sentence and try to make sense of the symbols. When you have done that, move on to the next sentence, then to the next section until you have interpreted all of the symbols.

When trying to interpret symbols, put on your detective hat and begin to ask yourself questions. Look at the symbols from every angle. Here are some main items to consider when interpreting the symbols.

Location

The location of a dream is very important. It sets the stage for the message that is being brought to your life. Ask yourself why the dream would be taking place where it is. The location of the dream is many times the key to unlocking an interpretation. Let's look at some examples.

If the dream takes place in a hospital, God may be speaking to you about your health, or maybe your job (if you work in a hospital). Or a dream in a bank may be God talking to you about your finances. A dream in the middle of the woods may talk about an area of your life that is lost. A dream on the beach may refer to rest and relaxation. Do you see how this works? One has to ponder carefully why the Holy Spirit would have the dream take place where it did. As you're looking at possible interpretations, pay attention to promptings in your spirit as many times the Holy Spirit will give you a witness that you're on the right track.

Perceptions

Many times, we'll have a certain perception within the dream as to its meaning. These perceptions are very important as they many times will unlock the meaning of the dream. Pay attention to them! After journaling your dream, leave some room underneath to include anything you sensed within your dream.

People

Remember, people are usually symbolic, and they do not represent themselves. They can represent themselves, but it is usually the exception and not the rule. Don't fall into the trap of always taking them literally; look at them symbolically. People are like the actors of a movie. Actors in movies do not represent themselves but the role that they are playing. Likewise, Aunt Sue may not be Aunt Sue; she may represent something else.

As you're trying to get the interpretation of what the person means, look at them symbolically. How would you describe that person? What is their personality like? What is their profession? By asking these questions, you are looking at possibilities of what they could mean. Then when you arrive at a possibility that makes sense to you, understand that what they represent is what God is addressing in your life.

I have a friend who is spiritually unstable. One day he wants to conquer the world for Christ and the next he is ready to turn his back on the Lord. For years my friend has always operated this way. I found out that whenever I struggled with instability in an area of my life, this friend would always begin to show up in my dreams. God was warning me of becoming like this friend. Unfortunately for my friend, the Holy Spirit was using him as a symbol of being unstable. That wasn't God's destiny for him, but God knew how to use him in a dream to speak to me of instability. What would God use you to represent? Hmm….interesting question, huh?

Basically, for technique #2, you are going to do your part to look at everything symbolically and you're going to attempt at arriving at a conclusion. Now, if you arrive at a conclusion but the dream doesn't fit your life anywhere now, leave your interpretation in place because it may fit your life down the line.

Technique #3 – Ask God the meaning of the dream.

Some of you may be thinking, "Why didn't we start off with this technique?" Well, I left it for last because we need to learn how to interpret symbols and how to look at dreams symbolically. In other words, we have to start attempting to take a "stab at it" and grow in our skill to interpret.

If none of the above has helped, take the dream that you have written into the presence of the Lord. Wait on His presence and spend time with Him. While you are pressing in, ask for the interpretation of the dream. It may come in a vision, a sense in your spirit, an audible voice or a God-thought. How it comes is not the part that we are looking to influence. Just open yourself before the Lord to hear however He chooses to speak.

I once had a dream that I could not interpret. Despite my many attempts to look at it symbolically and to fit it somewhere into my life, I remained unsuccessful. One early morning, I woke up and grabbed my dream journal and went down to the basement to pray. I prayed for a good while enjoying the Lord's presence. Suddenly I heard, "Open your dream journal." I immediately thought that the enemy was trying to distract me from my prayer time, so I ignored it. "Open your dream journal," the voice said again, and again I ignored it. Suddenly I was filled with an anointing so strong that I heard myself saying, "I said open your dream journal." By that time God had gotten my attention. I sat down and opened my dream journal to the dream that I was unsuccessful in interpreting. As I sat there ready for my next instruction, I began to hear faint words in my spirit. The Lord began to speak to me as to what each section meant and how it fit my life. He was revealing to me the direction that my ministry would take in the near future. Praise God. There will be times when God will be the one to give you the interpretation firsthand.

"What if I can't get the interpretation of the dream?"

Remember the previous statement that I made that not all dreams are God-given dreams. Some dreams will not have interpretations to them. That's a fact of the matter.

What I would recommend is that you write all of your dreams down. Don't try to discern beforehand if the dream is from God or not to determine if you're going to journal it. Journal all of your dreams! Now, if you know that the dream is a nightmare, don't journal those but follow the instructions that I listed under "Nightmares." All other dreams, write them in your journal. I love how my mentor Pastor Benny Thomas puts it: If in doubt, write it out! I believe that statement puts it very clear for us.

Our job is to get the dream down on paper before we forget it. It is easier for us to discern the dream after it is in written form.

Also, if you did get an interpretation for your dream but it doesn't seem to fit your life anywhere, that may be because it will be something that you'll need in the future. So for the dreams that you can't get an interpretation for or for those you interpret but don't fit, just put them on the side burner and let them stay there.

Review Your Journal Regularly

Get into the habit of reviewing your dream journal regularly. By doing so, many of the dreams that you could not interpret or did not fit will have had a chance to sit. As you wait for time to pass and then go back and re-read the dreams, many times it will be much easier to understand the symbolism.

It has occurred to me many times that dreams that have had a chance to sit have "jumped off the page" at me at a later time and have made sense later. Remember that some dreams will deal with future events. The reason why they may not fit is because the dream is addressing something that you'll be going through at a later time in life. That's why reviewing your journal is so critical. The answer you are waiting for may be sitting in one of your older journals.

I once woke up from a strange dream that had me puzzled. I dreamed that I was at a conference listening to a speaker. There was a break in the program for everyone to get refreshments. I was serving myself coffee when some people that I knew approached me and said to me, "We can't believe that you didn't come with us to launch our ministry." It was evident that they were all mad at me.

While I was rattled by their rudeness, I calmly but firmly replied, "I'm not called to launch that type of ministry." At that statement they were ready to get into an argument with me, so I was relieved when they announced that the workshop would continue. I left them and went and sat in my seat. The speaker got on the stage and said, "Okay, here's a teddy bear. I am going to throw it out into the crowd. Whoever catches it will be this conference's guest of honor and we will all have to treat them with special grace." As he threw out the teddy bear, I had a knowing that it was coming towards me. As I reached my hand out, I caught that teddy bear with barely any effort. I knew that the "mad crowd" would be even more upset, but I didn't care. I was enjoying my moment.

I woke up from that dream very perplexed. I had no idea whatsoever as to the meaning of the dream. I immediately looked into my life to see if I could find a fit. A year prior, I did receive an invitation from some friends to branch out and work on launching a specific type of ministry, but I declined being that I never quite felt called to do that. Even though that occurred a year prior, I didn't know how that dream related to my life at the present time. I told my wife about the dream and she gave me the same look of curiosity that I had. I wrote the dream down and went on about my day.

I went to my church where I worked to attend a staff meeting. As the staff meeting was taking place, I listened almost horrified as we were told that we would be moving toward launching the same type of ministry that I didn't feel called to. As the meeting progressed, my concerns continued to compound as I felt, once again, pressured to get involved launching that type of ministry.

After the meeting, I called my wife on the phone to ask for prayer. I shared with her the context of the meeting and my concerns. Then at one point in the conversation I said clearly, "I am not called to that type of ministry." When I said those words, the dream from the night prior jumped into my thoughts. That was the exact phrase that I used in the dream. Excitedly, I told my wife that I would have to call her back. Being that I didn't have the dream journal with me, I began to recall the dream. I was then able to see how it fit my life.

In the dream, I was being pressured to get involved with launching a certain type of ministry. After holding my ground and returning to my seat, I had caught the prize and was the guest of honor at the conference. Suddenly, the meaning of it burst forth in my thoughts. "By standing firm in your God-given call and not caving in to pressure, you will receive the prize of being honored by the Lord, even in the presence of those who are not convinced that you are on track." It all made sense. I was to stand firm in my own call and to be at rest and let the Lord make my call evident.

Interestingly enough, I never was approached by those at church to help launch that ministry. I was ready at any given moment to explain my call, but I never had to do it. God's grace was on me to walk in my call. Actually, I was given the green light to oversee the prophetic ministry of the church, which is the direction that I felt God calling me to.   In the midst of the church changing its outreach model, God told me to rest in my own call and He rewarded me for doing so.

In this example, God sent me a message in a dream ahead of time. After waking up, I couldn't find where this dream fit my life anywhere. As the day's events progressed, the message finally found the place to fit. This serves to inform you that not all dreams will fit your life when you have them. You may have to let them sit for a while so that they can fit later.

Symbols

We cannot develop our ability to hear the voice of God in dreams unless we start growing in our understanding of symbols. So, with that in mind, this next section will include some basic symbols for you to start with. The purpose of this section is to not give you a concrete list of symbols. These are some basic suggestions at what these symbols could mean. This is to help you get started. As you develop your own list of symbols with the Holy Spirit, you won't have to use these suggestions as much. This is only to help you get started.

Places

Bank: Your finances, your prosperity or your area of lack.

Hospital: Your health or your healing, literal or spiritual.

Jail: An area of bondage in your life; God talking about your deliverance.

School: A place of learning in your life.

Church   The Body of Christ as a whole; your actual church; your ministry.

Cemetery: An area of your life where things are dying – it could be the works of the flesh.

Amusement This could be an area of your life where you are
Park: being distracted; or an area where you are having a good time.

Your Home Just as you were born in your hometown, this could
Town: speak of an area in your life that is now being birthed.

Beach: Again, a place of distraction or a place of enjoyment and relaxation.

Theater: A place of entertainment; may speak of what you are entertaining yourself with.

Corn Field: May be speaking to you about harvest in your life.

Open Field: May be speaking to you about areas that are open to the Lord, or areas that He wants you to open.

People

Father: Father God; your actual father, his actual personality or your relationship with him; a spiritual mentor.

Mother: The Holy Spirit who is your Comforter; your actual mother, her personality or your relationship with her; a spiritual mentor.

Brother: Jesus who is a Friend that sticks closer than a brother; your actual brother, his personality or your relationship with him; a brother in Christ.

Sister: Your actual sister, her personality or your relationship with her; a sister in Christ.

Grand   Their influence on your life; the values that they
Parents: instilled into your life; your actual grandparents or their personalities.

(Note: Many people have shared their concern of dreaming about their deceased grandparents or parents. The concern comes from their talking with the dead in their dreams. Remember that these are only actors in a dream. They do not represent themselves in their dead state. They are a symbolic item in your dream. By looking at them symbolically, you will unlock the interpretation of the dream. Remember, if God was the one who forbade us to communicate with the deceased, He wouldn't break His own law by giving us dreams that violate His commandment. He is using them as a symbol to speak to us. Be free from your needless torment.)

Family   Ponder their personalities or your relationship with
Members: them to see if there is a symbolic link.

Pastor: The Lord; themselves or your relationship with them.

Boss: Someone in authority over you; your actual boss.

Police: Enforcing your authority.

Judge: The Lord who is your Judge; an area of your life where you are either judging or being judged.

Teacher: The Holy Spirit who is your Teacher; a mentor in your life.

Guest   For example, Kenneth Copeland may represent faith.

Guest Preachers: Joyce Meyer may represent teaching the word.

Benny Hinn may represent praying for the sick. T.D. Jakes may represent preaching the word. By looking at their types of ministries, you can understand what the guest preacher represents.

Things

Your Car: Your life; your family life.

Your House: Your life.

Living Room: Your daily living.

Dining Room: What you're feeding on.

Kitchen: Area of preparation.

Basement: Your foundation.

Your Bedroom: The intimate part of your life.

Bathroom: Areas of cleaning and purging.

Attic/Roof: Your thought life. What you spend time meditating on.

Backyard: Your past.

Backpack: Your burden; what you're carrying around.

Bus: Travel; your ministry.

Airplane: Travel; your ministry.

Tank: Spiritual warfare.

Bicycle: Balance.

Book: Learning and gaining knowledge; writing a book.

Angels: Messengers.

Weapon: Spiritual warfare; authority.

Storm: Trials and hardships; God is shaking the
                 shakable.

Rainbow: God's promises.

Animals

Eagles: The prophetic; being renewed; waiting on God.

Sharks: Being deceived by a deceiver; demonic plot to
                 deceive.

Friendly :   The Lord who sticks closer than a
Dogs   brother; friends.

Menacing   The devil looking to come against us.
Dogs:

Robins: Springtime – a season for new beginnings.

Fish: Souls being saved; a harvest.

Kangaroo: Being able to move quickly while carrying a ministry
                 or a project.

Snake: Deceiver; a plot of the devil.

Donkey: Service; humility.

Horse: Perseverance; able to run the distance without
                 growing weary.

Camel: Able to go the long distance with what the Lord put
                 in your spirit.

Colors

White:	Purity; holiness; or hanging on out of nervousness "white-knuckled".
Black:	Discreet; hidden; covered; or something evil.
Blue:	Revelatory realm; Holy Spirit.
Red:	The blood of Jesus; passion; or anger; bad temper.
Orange:	Fruit of the Spirit; or warning.
Green:	Life; growth; or envy.
Purple:	Royalty; majesty.

Puzzle Piece

Dreams are only one piece of the puzzle. They don't give you the whole picture in and of themselves. You'll need to combine what you receive in dreams with everything else that God shows you through the other ways that He speaks.

Never make a major life decision with what you received from the interpretation that you received in one dream. You'll need more pieces to put together an accurate picture of God's voice.

Remember, if He is speaking to you about a major life decision, He will be faithful to send you the other 2 or 3 witnesses so that you'll know that you're hearing accurately.

Let's move on now to the next puzzle piece.

-12 -
Night Visions
{Puzzle Piece #7}

"I was watching in the **night visions**, and behold, One like the Son of Man, Coming with the clouds of heaven!" Daniel 7:13 (emphasis mine)

What is a Night Vision?

As you read in the Bible, you'll notice that night visions were mentioned occasionally. As you read about them, it is easy to just assign them as another way of saying "dream". I've even heard people teach that night visions were dreams. Well, since the Bible doesn't make any distinguish between the two, it's just easy to assume that night visions are dreams.

Over time, however, I have encountered a certain strange phenomena that took place during the night season. Not being sure what to call it, I would try to describe it to people every time that it happened to me. I wasn't surprised when other believers also had the same experience or when I would even hear well-known ministers mention similar experiences. Over time, after prayer and searching the Scriptures and trying to make sense of these experiences, I have concluded that what I believe I had been experiencing were night visions.

The Bible specifically mentions dreams and the many times that God used them to talk to His people. So if a night vision were a dream, why not just call it a dream? Why specifically call it a night vision? Furthermore, a vision is something that you see while you are awake. A dream is something that you see while you are asleep. Does that mean that a night vision is something that you see at nighttime, say around 11pm or so? If a night vision were a dream, how could you be awake to see the vision? I know that I am splitting hairs, but I just want you to see the logic that I used to come to the obvious conclusion.

I have come to a conclusion that if a vision is something that you see while you are awake and a dream is something that you see while you're asleep, then a night vision is something that you see when you are in between being awake and being asleep.

An Active Spirit Realm

Whether you know it or not, our world is surrounded by an active spiritual realm. It is in this realm where angels and demons are constantly clashing in the ongoing spiritual warfare over cities, nations, and peoples. Furthermore, we are spirit beings that have a God-given discernment to understand what is taking place in the realm around us.

When we go to sleep, as we drift into and out of our sleep, I believe that we go into a phase where we are in the Spirit and are sensitive to hearing and seeing things from that spirit realm. Just as we're falling asleep, or right when we're waking up from our sleep, we may receive a night vision. I can usually tell if someone had a night vision because I'll ask them, "Were you awake or asleep?" They'll respond, "I don't know. I had lain down to go to sleep and was not yet fully asleep when I saw a vision."

In that place between being awake and asleep, God will speak His words to us so that we can hear His voice. Let's look at the types of revelations that take place on this level.

Visions

In this "in-between" place, you may see visions. When you do, you should treat this the same way that you treat a vision that you see while you're awake. It is so important to not only recall your dreams, but to try to recall if you have seen a vision either before or after sleeping.

I once had a dream in which I heard a voice telling me the interpretation throughout the dream. I was wondering to myself whose voice was speaking the interpretation to me. As I was waking up from the dream and was not yet fully awake, I suddenly saw the face of Jesus projected on one of the walls in my room. He was smiling at me as to say, "I gave you the interpretation of your dream." Just as I became fully awake, His face vanished from the wall. It was in that in-between place that I saw the Lord and knew He had given me a sure interpretation.

These night visions may be a picture that you see or maybe even a movie-like scene playing before your eyes. Just write down what you see and refer to the chapter on visions for instructions on how to understand their symbolic nature and how to interpret them.

Some examples of what you could see in night visions are:

~ The Lord.
~ Angels.
~ Somebody trying to wake you up.
~ Any kind of animal in your room.
~ A person speaking a message to you.
~ A Bible flipping open to a certain Scripture.
~ A geographical place.

The options are limitless. God can use any kind of image to speak to you in a night vision.

Sounds

Oh, yes...just because it's called night visions doesn't limit the revelation to only sights. Sounds are also included in this category. After all, look at what happened to Israel in his night vision.

> *"Then God spoke to Israel in the visions of the night, and said, 'Jacob, Jacob!' And he said, 'Here I am.'" Genesis 46:2*

God spoke to Israel in the visions of the night. The night visions are not only limited to sights and visions, you may also hear sounds that speak to you while you are in that in-between realm of half asleep and half awake.

Music

Music is a regular sound that God uses to speak in night visions. I have often said in my classes that if you have a dream and as you're waking up from that dream you hear a song, that song contains the key to your interpretation. Don't think that God will only use gospel music to speak to you. Remember, He is a wise God who will use even the things of this world for His purposes.

One cold winter, my wife and I took a vacation with my spiritual mentors, Pastors Benny & Sandy Thomas. As we enjoyed several days of beauty in the Thousand Islands, we were also pressing in to God for guidance regarding the ministry.

One morning Pastor Benny excitedly shared a dream he had the night prior in which God was clarifying to him the next steps to take in the ministry. I listened in awe and as he finished I asked, "Did God mention a time frame to you?" Pastor Benny chuckled and said, "Interesting that you ask that. As I was waking up from the dream, I was hearing a record playing in my room. It was the song by Elvis Presley, "It's Now or Never." Through that song in a night vision as he was waking up from a dream, Pastor Benny was able to receive the time frame for applying the revelation.

On another occasion, I had a dream in which God was speaking to me about how we discount His voice when it comes through a dream. As I was waking up from this dream, I heard a song from when I was a teenager. The artist was Debbie Gibson and the song was called, "Only in My Dreams." I actually heard the line from the chorus playing and the words were, "No, only in my dreams. As real as it may seem, it was only in my dreams." God was putting His finger on an area of unbelief that many walk in. Being that I was currently teaching a class on Hearing the Voice of God in Dreams, He was exposing to me the problem of why many people are not successful at hearing His voice in the night season. God in His wisdom, picked through all of the songs that I had been exposed to in my life and used one that would get His message across. How cool is that?

People

You may hear people talking and overhear a conversation. Or you may hear someone calling your name. God may use any of those scenarios to talk to you.

Other Noises

You may hear a phone ringing in a night vision, which could mean that God is calling you and trying to get your attention. I remember once being wakened by my cell phone that was ringing non-stop next to my bed. I finally woke up and reached over to grab it only to discover that there was no cell phone there. Yet again, God had gotten my attention.

You may hear someone knocking on your door or walking around in your house. Remember when I mentioned earlier that God used to wake me up at 3:33 a.m. to go and pray? Well, He would always use the most unconventional methods to wake me. One early morning as I was in a deep sleep, I heard the footsteps of a man walking in my hall right outside my bedroom. How I knew the footsteps belonged to a man is well beyond me. I just knew. I woke up with my heart racing! I wasn't fearful, I actually felt exhilarated as in my spirit I sensed that it was a good thing. I never did get to see the messenger who woke me, but it was not uncommon for God to use angels to give wake up calls.

"Now the angel who talked with me came back and wakened me, as a man who is wakened out of his sleep." Zechariah 4:1

Here are some other sounds that you may hear in night visions:

~ The television loudly blaring a program.
~ Airplanes flying nearby.
~ Words being spoken to you that seem to come from nowhere.
~ Someone laughing or crying.

These options are also limitless as God can use any sound to speak to you.

Touches

In this category, your sense of touch would be used to communicate a message to you in a night vision. You may feel something being placed on you like a mantle or feel someone measuring you like a tailor as you lay still.

Going through a difficult time in the ministry, I was praying to God for strength. As I was ready to retire for the night one evening, I went up to my bedroom. My wife was downstairs taking care of a few things and, not wanting to go to sleep until she had joined me, I turned on the news in my room to watch in the interim. Although I was watching the news, my mind was on the problem that I was going through in the ministry. Without wanting to, I quickly drifted off to sleep while I was lying flat on my back. About 20 minutes later, I could hear my wife enter the room, getting ready to go to bed. Suddenly, as I was waking up, I became aware of something wedged behind me. While I had fallen asleep flat on my back, something was under me, and I was now leaning completely on my right side. My first thought was that my daughter Alyssa had crawled behind me somehow and it was she who was lodged behind me. Being half-asleep and half-awake, I looked behind me only to see these two BIG transparent hands that were placed on my back and were holding me to one side. Quickly, I tried making sense out of what I was seeing, because in my foggy state of mind, I couldn't grasp what was going on. Suddenly, a knowing downloaded into my spirit and I knew that God was answering my prayer and letting me know that while I was going through my difficult times in ministry, He would be faithful to uphold me. Praise God! Shortly after I became fully awake and the hands disappeared. I told my wife what happened with the little bit of strength I had before falling back to sleep. Just as He revealed through that prophetic touch, God was faithful, and He did walk me through the dark days ahead as I navigated some discouraging things in the ministry. I continued to look back and remember that He promised to uphold me.

Smells

Our God is the God of fragrances. He loves to express who He is and what He is doing through fresh fragrances that speak volumes to us. Do you know that one smell can speak volumes to you? It is possible to remember a whole part of your life with only one smell. It may be a perfume you used or a cologne, or a spice that you used regularly in your food. Smells are powerful messengers.

Be aware of smells in your night visions. Journal them and ponder their significance. What could God speak through the scent of vanilla? Rosemary? Flowers? Cinnamon? It would be an adventure to find out what He's saying.

Tastes

Last, but definitely not least, we have tastes. God gave us a sense of taste so that we could use our taste buds to discern between what is bitter and sweet and sour and bland. He can also give us specific tastes that speak to us.

If there is one feeling that I find very uncomfortable it is the feeling of heartburn. I don't have it anymore as a result of prayer, praise God, but I have had my uncomfortable bouts with heartburn. Therefore, I was not surprised when God began to use the symptom of heartburn to speak to me.

I would have a recurring experience in a night vision that I did not understand. As I was in that in-between place of being asleep and awake, I would at times have this taste in my mouth that would cause me to experience heartburn. I would even wake up at times with that strange taste in my mouth. It was not a taste that I enjoyed, and it wasn't something that I ate before going to bed. I normally would just ignore it and go brush my teeth hoping not to have to taste that yucky flavor again.

It took me a while before I even gave it a second thought that it might be prophetic. Just as the symptom is called "heartburn," God may have been speaking to me about my "heart being burned" or being betrayed. Looking back, I find it amazing the accuracy between the taste in the night vision and when I had to walk through difficult places in relationships. Had I made the connection sooner, I probably would have known how to pray over these "friendships" and might have avoided some painful situations.

A Little Far-Fetched?

Do you think that this is a little far-fetched? Well, if you do, I would recommend that you read the Bible. For in it you find the strangest accounts of God speaking through a donkey, God transporting a man from the desert to another city by the Spirit, another man running faster than horses, etc.

God is the God of the impossible. He can do anything that He wants and will use methods outside of our paradigms to speak to us.

Let's get God out of the box that we've put Him in and allow Him to communicate to us.

What to do with Night Visions?

When you have these night visions, journal them down in your dream journal. If you had the night vision waking up from a dream, it may be the key to interpreting your dream. If you just had the night vision and no dream, treat it as a stand-alone piece of revelation.

Just as visions, night visions can be symbolic or literal. It is usually more literal when a voice or someone speaks to you directly. Otherwise, if the night vision is more surreal, look at it symbolically to understand its meaning.

An Answer of Peace

I cannot finish this chapter without sharing an account of something that happened to me.

I was once invited to attend a very controversial meeting for the Hispanic community of my city. I had a sense of responsibility to attend, although I didn't feel at peace about it in my spirit. For reasons I won't get into in this book, I was requested by name to personally be at this meeting and to speak my thoughts about the controversial situation. I knew that if I didn't attend, some community leaders would be upset with me as I had previously committed myself to attending. However, I had a suspicion that going to this meeting to give my thoughts would not help the solution, but would actually only make the problem worse. Feeling torn up about it, I pressed into prayer.

As the night before the meeting came, I was still in my prayer closet going back and forth about what to do in this situation. Suddenly, a fleeting thought came out of nowhere, "Call your mother and ask for her opinion." At first I thought it was a distraction, but being willing to test it, I called her. She did not answer the phone when I called. Being that it was getting late, I decided I would go to bed and give it one last try in the morning.

As soon as I woke up, I made my way downstairs and called my mother again. This time she answered the phone. "Hello," she answered. "Hi, Mom, it's me, Hector. I want to ask you your opinion about something." "Okay," she responded.

So I took about 4 minutes to explain the situation that was before me and the decision that I had to make. As soon as I finished, she said, "Okay, well, first of all, I was expecting your call."

"You were expecting my call? What do you mean?" I responded shocked.

"Well, let me tell you what happened to me this morning. I woke up around 5 a.m. and went to the living room to lie down on the sofa. I hadn't fully drifted to sleep when suddenly a man was standing in my living room. He said to me, 'When Hector calls you this morning, tell him not to go.' So that's why I knew that you would be calling, and I already know the answer that you need to hear."

I was very excited that God had once again given me the necessary direction that I needed. This time it came through a night vision that my mother had. Praise God!

I'm glad that my mother believed in God's communication and that she didn't throw out what she saw as her imagination. She could have ruined the flow of communication that God had for me had she been an unbeliever. How I thank God she didn't.

As a result, I contacted the community person and made it clear that I was not going to go to the meeting. I wasn't the most liked guy after not going to the meeting. I didn't care. I knew that God had given me my answer of peace. I also realized much later that the person planning this meeting only wanted me there to serve his purposes. I couldn't have seen that beforehand, but I'm grateful that God can see all of the motivations of the heart.

One Piece of the Puzzle

Night visions are only one piece of the puzzle. They go hand in hand with all of the other pieces. Never make a major life decision only on what you see, hear, feel, smell or taste in a night vision. Press into God for confirmations. Let's move on to the next puzzle piece.

-13 -
Prophetic Events, Signs & Circumstances
{Puzzle Piece #8}

"For in Him we live and move and have our being." Acts 17:28

Up to this point, we have talked about methods that God uses to speak to us while we are praying, dreaming, or resting. With this chapter, we are now going to begin exploring how God speaks to our lives when we are going about our days.

As believers, our lives are more supernatural than we think. We must give God some glory to know that He is always involved in the details that surround our lives. After all, He cares about us. As a father, I'm concerned about the details in my daughters' lives such as their homework being done and their rooms being clean. I'm concerned because I love them and want them to have the best in life. In like manner, God cares for us. It's awesome that while He governs over the universe, He cares about each one individually and will even get involved in every detail of our lives.

Our Praying Releases Answers from Heaven

The word establishes the precedent that God responds to us as a result of prayer. Daniel was concerned about the future of his people and took this to the Lord in prayer. Let's read the account.

> *"In the third year of Cyrus king of Persia, a revelation was given to Daniel (who was called Belteshazzar). Its message was true and it concerned a great war. The understanding of the message came to him in a vision. At that time I, Daniel, mourned for three weeks. I ate no choice food; no meat or wine touched my lips; and I used no lotions at all until the three weeks were over. On the twenty-fourth day of the first month, as I was standing on the bank of the great river, the Tigris, I looked up and there before me was a man dressed in linen, with a belt of the finest gold around his waist. His body was like chrysolite, his face like lightning, his eyes like flaming torches, his arms and legs like the gleam of burnished bronze, and his voice like the sound of a multitude. I, Daniel, was the only one who saw the vision; the men with me did not see it, but such terror overwhelmed them that they fled and hid themselves.*

So I was left alone, gazing at this great vision; I had no strength left, my face turned deathly pale and I was helpless. Then I heard him speaking, and as I listened to him, I fell into a deep sleep, my face to the ground. A hand touched me and set me trembling on my hands and knees. He said, 'Daniel, you who are highly esteemed, consider carefully the words I am about to speak to you, and stand up, for I have now been sent to you.' And when he said this to me, I stood up trembling. Then he continued, 'Do not be afraid, Daniel. **Since the first day that you set your mind to gain understanding and to humble yourself before your God, your words were heard, and I have come in response to them.** *But the prince of the Persian kingdom resisted me twenty-one days. Then Michael, one of the chief princes, came to help me, because I was detained there with the king of Persia.* **Now I have come to explain to you what will happen to your people in the future, for the vision concerns a time yet to come.'"** *Daniel 10:1-14* (emphasis mine)

Let me ask you a question. When was Daniel's answer released to him? When the angel spoke with him? No! The angel told Daniel that since the *first day that he set his mind to understand, his words were heard and the angel was sent as a response to them.* What can we take from that? From the moment that we set our hearts to understand and to humble ourselves before the Lord in prayer, He responds. We have to make a connection between praying and watching for God's answer to come in whatever way He chooses to send it.

So, as you approach God in prayer and ask Him to respond to you, remember to use your detective anointing to search for the answer that God sends your way. Keep journaling your dreams, night visions, visions, God-thoughts, spirit impressions and promptings and be faithful to review the journal to look for your clues. There is something else that you need to be made aware of – look for prophetic events that take place in your day.

Prophetic Events

What if I told you that God enjoys acting out something to speak to you? It would be as if God sets up a skit that was designed to provide your answer. The only thing is that you have to use your detective anointing to discern it, or you could easily pass it by and not notice it. Let's get a biblical example.

> "This is the word that came to Jeremiah from the LORD: Go down to the potter's house, and there I will give you my message. So I went down to the potter's house, and I saw him working at the wheel. But the pot he was shaping from the clay was marred in his hands; so the potter formed it into another pot, shaping it as seemed best to him. **Then the word of the LORD came to me**..."
> Jeremiah 18:1-5 (emphasis mine)

How did God speak to the prophet Jeremiah? Did He give him a vision, or did Jeremiah hear an audible voice? Neither. Jeremiah had to go to the potter's house, and when he got there, he had to watch what the potter was doing. Through what he was observing, God spoke to Jeremiah. So let's look at it this way. God had set up a skit and was arranging for it to be played out in front of Jeremiah. He had Jeremiah go to the potter's house to see the play, which would provide the picture of what God was saying. God used the visual picture of the potter's activity in designing the pot of clay to speak a spiritual message to Jeremiah and to Israel.

Many times as a result of prayer, God also sets up prophetic events in our day to speak a message to us. Just like God spoke to Jeremiah at the potter's house, He is setting up a skit to speak to you. That is precisely why we should go through life aware that God sets things up all around us to talk to us. It would be foolish to ignore our surroundings and to move mechanically through life.

Can you imagine how frustrated the angels get when you don't recognize God's voice in your surroundings? We pray for an answer from God. He responds and sends the angels to set up prophetic events in our day. We walk through the prophetic event that was designed by God to speak to us, and we don't discern His voice. The angels probably say, "Aww, he missed it again." It doesn't have to be that way. Just decide to develop your skill to watch for prophetic events in your day, and you can get better at it.

I remember a training that I took to become a security guard. I was a newlywed and was working part-time and studying in college part-time. I had to take on a new part-time job to help ends meet. I found a job close to my home as a security guard on the weekends. The hardest part of the training that I encountered was the part of being observant. As a security guard, we had to report light bulbs that had burned out, fire extinguishers that had expired and suspicious activity anywhere. That required a constant state of vigilance that I was not accustomed to. Despite all of the rules that I learned, I only improved in this area after time and practice. Some people are more vigilant by nature and will not have a hard time activating themselves to hear from God through prophetic events that occur in their days. If you are not vigilant by nature, don't despair. You can make up your mind to develop yourself over time.

A God-given Mentor

Previously, I have mentioned how I have a God-given mentor that has been instrumental in my life. When I first learned about Pastor Benny Thomas and his ministry, I was blessed with his method of teaching. Shortly afterward, I was praying one day thanking God for all that I was learning through his ministry. Suddenly in my spirit, I heard these words, "You will work with him."

"Work with him?" I questioned. "I don't even know him."

"Leave the introductions to Me," was the response I received.

Shortly afterward, I sent a letter to Pastor Thomas' office thanking him for the wonderful teaching ministry. I never expected a response of any kind. However, about a year later, as I was working in my office at the church, I received a call from him. As I went to answer the phone, a voice whispered in my ear, *"Pastor Benny Thomas."*

"Hello, this is Hector. May I help you?" I answered.

"Hello, Hector, this is Pastor Benny Thomas." I was shocked. Just as God had promised, He set up a time for our introductions. That was the beginning of a great friendship over several years. Eventually, we invited him to come and speak at my local church, and he did.

Now by this time, I had been asking the Lord for a mentor to help me in ministry and was staying alert for His response. Being that I really appreciated Pastor Thomas, it was just natural for me to wonder if he was the answer to my prayer. Actually, I thought it was more wishful thinking. I wondered if he was too busy to help me; not to mention that I lived in New York and he resided in Texas.

On one visit to New York, we set up the plan to go on vacation together to the Thousand Islands. Pastor Benny and his wife Sandy, and my wife Barbie and I enjoyed having the Thousand Islands to ourselves being that we went during an off-season. One day we decided to go into Canada for some shopping. We spent a glorious day in Kingston, Ontario, shopping and taking in the scenery. As late afternoon approached, we decided that we would head back to the States.

As we approached the Border Patrol to re-enter into the United States, the Border Police told us, "You have been selected for a random search." My heart sank because I felt responsible for my guest from Texas. Now, we had no reason to be nervous, but I was nervous nonetheless. Visions of refugees hanging on the rented car's muffler began to play about in my mind.

"Head of households, please step forward," the officer at the desk spoke authoritatively. Pastor Thomas and I took one step forward. "Please fill out these forms and let us know what you have in your bags in the car." We took 10 minutes or so filling out the form. When we were done, we were asked to have a seat and wait for our vehicle to be inspected.

It was like torture waiting there for the inspection to be done. Finally, one officer walks in and says out loud, "We have a problem!" My heart sank from my stomach to my kneecaps. After he so "kindly" vocalized that there was a problem, he then went over to another group of officers and began to whisper. I wanted to shout out to them, "Well, what is the problem?" As they left us there in our agony, they went back out to the car to search some more. Ten minutes later they re-entered the building.

Finally, a supervisor spoke out loud to the other officers. "I found the mistake." He had the attention of both officers and my group of four. "The mistake is that you have entered them into our computer as two families in one car. You are supposed to enter them as one family in one car." As soon as he said those words, he turned to us and said, "Folks, you are all set," as he handed us the car keys. Walking out of that place, the gravity of what just happened fell on me. In my prayers to find a spiritual mentor, I had wondered if God had sent me Pastor Thomas. Then, he acted out in front of me a scenario that confirmed that we were supposed to be as one family. God had brought us together! God had sent Jeremiah to the potter's house to talk to him there, but He sent me to the Border Patrol. Since then, we have become like family as God had ordained.

"From English to Spanish"

There was another time when I had offered to translate into Spanish a book that Pastor Thomas had written. I knew God had put it in my heart, but I also realized the huge time commitment that was involved in undertaking such a task. I was asking God for a confirmation before actually jumping in completely.

On this different trip that the Thomases took to New York, my wife and I took them to Canada again. This time we took them to Niagara Falls to enjoy the ambiance around the Niagara Falls. It was winter again, so despite the fact that the wind chill was below zero and that we could only glance at the falls for a few moments before having to run indoors, the view was breathtaking.

Shortly afterward, we settled into the back of a coffee shop to warm up with a nice hot cup of coffee. The shop was particularly empty on that night, and our party of four decided to sit at a table at the farthest corner near the back; the furthest distance from the counter.

As we all sipped the comforting hot beverage, Pastor Thomas, in a very low voice, casually asked, "Hector, have you given any more thought to translating the book into Spanish?" The volume of his voice was so low that although I was sitting across the table from him, I almost didn't hear him. Right at that precise moment when he asked me the question, from the front of the store, suddenly we hear a voice shout out loudly, " From English to Spanish!" As we all turned around to see who shouted that phrase, we spotted the two coffee shop employees. The one who had blurted the phrase looked completely embarrassed as he had his hand covered over his mouth. The other employee softly mouthed the words "I'm sorry" to us apologizing for the interruption. These two employees had been goofing around and somehow forgot that we were in the store until they looked back and saw us there.

I don't know what they were talking about that made the young man blurt out such a phrase. Nonetheless, to us, we had just witnessed a prophetic event in which God confirmed to me the taking on of this task. The precise time when we heard the young man shout those words was exactly when Pastor Thomas had asked me about the project. The timing was impeccable. I knew it was a God set-up because there was no way that they could have heard Pastor Thomas ask me that question with such a low voice at such a far distance. Only God could have worked out that event so prophetically.

I did end up translating the book for Pastor Thomas, and I'm sure that it will be a major blessing in the lives of those who read it.

How to Watch for Prophetic Events

Prophetic events occur more than most of us know. Many are not aware that this method to hear from God exists. For those who will activate their senses to hear from God this way, you will pick up a whole bunch of communication. Usually, when people tell me that they prayed about something and have not heard from God, I assure them that God had most likely responded, but the hindrance lied more in their lack of knowing how to discern God's voice.

A prophetic event is basically an event in your day that God sets up to communicate to you. All day long we go through our days observing and witnessing events that once we walk away from, we don't remember anymore.

Here is a question that you could ask yourself that would help you consider events as a prophetic event. As you observe happenings in your day that catch your attention, ask yourself, "Could God be speaking to me through this?" This question helps you stay sensitive to what you are watching and will encourage you to look at events prophetically. So rather than just looking at the event literally, look beyond the literal level and search to see if God acted out a prophetic message for you.

I once woke up late for work and rushed through my morning duties to hurry up and get to my office. As I was driving to my office, I remember feeling drained and exhausted. I prayed on my way to work, but still I noticed that something was missing. I felt...tired! As I pulled up to my office building, I reversed into my parking spot (my usual custom), which allowed me to face the street. As I sat there, I asked God what was wrong with me and why I felt so drained. Suddenly, a huge truck drove past that had the word "POWER" displayed on its side. As I observed the truck, it did a U-Turn right in front of me and went back the other way from which it had come. Had I not activated my senses as an Anointed Detective, I would not have picked up the message. Fortunately for me, I knew God was telling me to go back and get my power. As a routine, I would pray in the Holy Spirit every morning and spend time getting spiritually ready for my day. Being that I woke up late, I neglected to do this and as a result, I felt tired and drained. I knew God was answering my prayer and telling me that I needed to fuel up for the day with power. So I went into my office, closed the door and prayed to be refueled with power from on high. God acted out the prophetic message to me through a power truck that did a U-Turn in front of me. I know that as a result of my prayers the angels had to have the truck ready to drive past my office and at the right time they had it do a U-Turn. Think about how detailed this was; God had to coordinate quite a bit to get me to observe a prophetic event designed to speak to me. He does that all the time to us, and we can activate our senses to identify these prophetic events.

Prophetic Events Seem Like Natural Events

As you're looking to hear from God through prophetic events, understand that they seem like regular, normal events so much that it is easy to ignore what we have seen. We must look intentionally at all of our day's events through a prophetic magnifying glass to capture those events that are prophetic.

Let me clarify that not all events we encounter are God-events. He knows that we have a life to live. We have to work, we have to cook, we have to pay bills, we have to take our children to their soccer practice. He wouldn't speak so much that we couldn't focus on our responsibilities. However, we have gone to the other side of the extreme. We are guilty of focusing so much on our responsibilities that we don't look for the voice of God. God will set you up with prophetic events to communicate to you, but you have to be on your watch.

Look for the Timing of Prophetic Events

When praying for an answer, the time to start watching carefully for prophetic events is right after you're done praying. Remember that your answer is sent when you set your heart to understand and humble yourself before God. Now, walk in your detective anointing and be vigilant throughout your day for prophetic events. Timing is key to recognizing these God set-ups. My advice to you is: pray, then watch!

Signs

Signs are all over the place in the natural realm. There are signs that tell us the numbers on the highways, the names of the streets, and the traffic signs tell us when to stop, yield or merge. It is by reading these signs that we know where to drive, what speed to drive, where to park, etc.

The same occurs in the spiritual realm. There are signs that God will prophetically place in your path to speak a rhema (living) word to you. When you are walking in the Spirit and being led by the Spirit, He will lead you to places where signs will speak His words to you.

A sign, in essence, is another way to call a prophetic event. It is something that God places before you to speak a message to you. These aren't only literal signs that God can use, but anything out of your regular day that could give you a clear message.

> *"In the year that Tartan came to Ashdod, when Sargon the king of Assyria sent him, and he fought against Ashdod and took it, at the same time the LORD spoke by Isaiah the son of Amoz, saying, 'Go, and remove the sackcloth from your body, and take your sandals off your feet.' And he did so, walking naked and barefoot. Then the LORD said, 'Just as My servant Isaiah has walked naked and barefoot three years for a sign and a wonder against Egypt and Ethiopia, so shall the king of Assyria lead away the Egyptians as prisoners and the Ethiopians as captives, young and old, naked and barefoot, with their buttocks uncovered, to the shame of Egypt.'" Isaiah 20:1-5 (emphasis mine)*

Yes, you read that correctly. God provided a sign against Egypt and Ethiopia. What was the sign? He had the prophet Isaiah walk around naked and barefoot for *three years!* During that timeframe, whenever Isaiah was spotted walking around naked and barefoot, it was a sign to remind the people of what God was saying against Egypt and Ethiopia.

God really is creative when it comes to providing a sign that speaks. He can use anything to communicate a word to us, including signs, people, animals, etc. God is creative. We have to function as Anointed Detectives to pick up on it.

I was praying in my office regarding a ministry opportunity that had opened up to me. As much as I wanted to accept it, I had a fear in the pit of my stomach every time I thought about it. I knew that the fear I was experiencing was coming from a place of feeling inadequate. I was battling thoughts of doubt regarding my ability to follow through successfully with this ministry event. I knew that God was with me, but the bigness of the opportunity was intimidating me. As I was praying in my office and asking God to speak to me, I happened to look out of my office window, which overlooks a busy highway. At that precise moment, a huge truck drove by with enormous letters that read, "YOU CAN DO IT!" I instantly felt comforted and encouraged. I knew I had received the word of the Lord. God spoke to me through a sign...literally.

The difference between a prophetic event and a sign is that a prophetic event is an *event.* Something that happens to you or around you that speaks to you. A sign is something that you behold or hear that speaks to you. It doesn't necessarily have to be an event. I used two truck examples that God has used to speak to me. In one example, I observed a truck that said "Power" do a U-Turn. That was a prophetic event because the part that God was highlighting to me was not only the words on the truck, but also what the truck did: a U-Turn. In the other example, God used words "YOU CAN DO IT!" on a truck to speak to me. The truck didn't do anything that was prophetic. It was just the signage that God was highlighting. In essence, it doesn't really matter if you can recall the difference between the two. It's just important to be aware and catch what God is saying.

After going to a service where a well-known prophet was speaking, my family was in the car driving home. We were sharing about the powerful prophetic words the prophet had declared regarding multiplication. He had declared it over everyone in the meeting and also exhorted us to have faith for immediate manifestation. Deep into that conversation, I pulled the car into our driveway and stopped abruptly before going all the way in. Surprised at my sudden halt, my wife asked, "What's wrong?" I replied, "Look on our lawn." Then she spotted it. There in the dark sitting on our front lawn was a beautiful white rabbit. We have never seen rabbits in our area and much less on our front lawn. But there it was, hoping to escape detection. Excited to see it, my daughters let out a loud laugh and scared it away. My wife and I looked at each other and had a knowing look. God had used rabbits in our dreams before to speak symbolically of multiplication. Here was a sign in the natural of what we were believing God for in the spiritual.

This kind of scenario happens all the time. Consider what you are going through and what you are asking God for in prayer. Then look at the timing of when you run into certain animals. God can use the animal's characteristics to speak to you of what He is saying. Learn to look at animals symbolically and a whole new world of hearing God's voice in signs will open up to you.

I've already shared in a previous chapter about an inconsistent friend of mine. Just as he was inconsistent in his walk with the Lord, whenever I was becoming inconsistent, this friend would appear in my dreams. I began to realize, however, that God was using something other than my dreams. While I lost touch with this friend, it was supernatural how I would run into him when God was telling me to remain consistent. It was as if God was using him as a sign of inconsistency. I would run into him at the post office, I would see him walking down the street, and I even once saw him across from me at the traffic light. The amazing thing was that when I did see him, God had recently used him in my dream to talk to my life. That caught my attention as I soon realized that symbolism continues even after we wake up from our dreams. God can and will use what people mean symbolically to talk to you.

Now don't let that upset you. Some may think that God is unfair because He is using this person to represent inconsistency. It's not that God wants him to stay that way; God always has our best in mind. Remember, being that God was speaking to me, He was using a symbol of my own vocabulary to represent inconsistency. God knew that I had those thoughts toward my friend, and He used it for His purposes. Our God is a Master at using everything for His purposes.

When God does use people as a sign to you, you will know it because what they represent will fit what God is saying to you through other methods. One way to pick up His message is to ask yourself, "How would I describe this person?" It may be his personality that God is using to speak to you. Or it may be his career, or some other thing. Learn to think symbolically.

When seeking the Lord, be aware of signs that are speaking to you the word of the Lord.

Circumstances

> "Nevertheless, lest we offend them, go to the sea, cast in a hook, and take the fish that comes up first. And when you have opened its mouth, you will find a piece of money; take that and give it to them for Me and you." Matthew 17:27

Reading the above Scripture, we see that Jesus gave Peter a clear directive as to where to go and find money to pay for the temple tax. They had just arrived to Capernaum, and the tax collectors were looking to make sure that Jesus paid the temple tax. So they cornered Peter and asked him about it. Peter assured them that Jesus would pay the tax. The Bible says that even before Peter mentioned the matter to Jesus, Jesus already knew what was going on and told Peter where to go and get the money to pay the tax.

While Matthew left the story there, we have to assume that as Peter followed Jesus' instructions, everything panned out exactly as Jesus had foretold. Being that one of Jesus' ministries was that of Prophet, it was required that everything that He prophesied and foretold came to pass. God had previously established that requirement from Prophets that were to speak in Israel.

> "And if you say in your heart, 'How shall we know the word which the LORD has not spoken?'— **when a prophet speaks in the**

name of the LORD, if the thing does not happen or come to pass, that *is* the thing which the LORD has not spoken; the prophet has spoken it presumptuously; you shall not be afraid of him." Deuteronomy 18:21-22 (emphasis mine)

Therefore, we must assume that everything Jesus told Peter through the word of wisdom, occurred exactly as He had foretold it. This is just one of the many examples of Jesus giving direct guidance from revelation knowledge that came to pass in the natural realm.

Another example is when Jesus told His disciples where to let down their nets for a big catch.

> *"When He had stopped speaking, He said to Simon, '**Launch out into the deep and let down your nets for a catch.**' But Simon answered and said to Him, '**Master, we have toiled all night and caught nothing; nevertheless at Your word I will let down the net.**' And when they had done this, they caught a great number of fish, and their net was breaking. So they signaled to their partners in the other boat to come and help them. And they came and filled both the boats, so that they began to sink.** When Simon Peter saw it, he fell down at Jesus' knees, saying, 'Depart from me, for I am a sinful man, O Lord!' **For he and all who were with him were astonished at the catch of fish which they had taken...**"* Luke 5:4-9 (emphasis mine)

Jesus was so accurate with His revelation knowledge that Peter was left astonished. Peter fell on his face and asked the Lord to depart from Him. I would imagine that Peter had never experienced such a powerful demonstration of the word of the Lord in his life.

Of what value would it have been if Jesus gave Peter the directive of where to go fish only for him not to find any? Or of telling Peter where to find the money for the temple tax and for the fish to turn up empty? It would have been of no value. In order for there to be a prophetic significance, the circumstances had to unfold just as Jesus said they would.

As God speaks to our lives and leads us toward our destinies, our present circumstances should line up with what He is saying. This is one of the methods of testing the revelation that God is giving you. When God tells you that something will occur, it should. There are various reasons why we may run into some problems with our circumstances not lining up.

Maybe We Didn't Hear Accurately

We have to make room for us to know that we may have missed it. Despite our hearing God in the many ways He speaks and regardless of our effort to journal what we receive, we are still human beings with emotions and can miss it at times. The more we develop our skill in hearing God, however, the more we can see a reduction of the times that we miss it and celebrate more victories when we understand and walk in God's plan for our lives.

Timing

Timing is another important piece of the puzzle. As we receive revelation from God, He will be faithful to tell us when to implement that revelation. As we step out in His timing, the circumstances should line up with His word. If we step in and the circumstances are not lined up, maybe we have misjudged the timing.

Our Circumstances Should Fit the Puzzle

Ideally, our circumstances should fit the revelation that we've received from God. That is a good way to confirm what you have been hearing accurately. If for some reason the circumstances are not lined up, do not fall under condemnation. Go before the Lord in prayer and let Him speak to you on how to move forward.

One Piece of the Puzzle

That's right. Just as we've concluded all other methods of God's voice, the puzzle pieces discussed in this chapter are not stand-alone pieces; they need to go with the other pieces. Who can take one piece of a puzzle and then say that they've solved the whole puzzle? They can't. It'd be foolish. You need *all* pieces of a puzzle to fit together snugly to give the full picture.

Do not make any life decisions on what you've picked up through prophetic events, signs or your circumstances. You'll need to add other puzzle pieces to get confirmation. Let's move on.

-14 -
Other Creative Methods
{Puzzle Piece #9}

"For who has known the mind of the Lord? Or who has become His counselor?" Romans 11:34

Let God Be God

Our finite minds cannot comprehend God in the fullness of His glory. God is just too big to fit in one little brain. Therefore, apart from what He has revealed to us already, we cannot say that we know everything about God. We don't! There is yet so much for us to learn about Him.

> *"The secret things belong to the LORD our God, but those things which are revealed belong to us and to our children forever, that we may do all the words of this law."* Deuteronomy 29:29

God in His wisdom reveals only what He knows we need and can grasp with our limited capacities. Therefore, we have things that are revealed and other things that are still mysteries. The above Scripture establishes the principle that the revealed things are for us and the mysteries belong to the Lord.

We should appreciate, value and cherish everything that He has shown to us. On the same note, we should respect and leave alone those things that are secret and that God has chosen not to reveal. There will be some things left unexplained leaving us forced to wait until we enter into eternity to inquire further.

My purpose in making this point is to highlight the fact that there are things that God will do, things He will say and methods He will use that make no sense to us. So, in essence, we must all come to the agreement that we have to let God be God. Don't tell God how to speak to you and, more importantly, don't tell God the ways that He can speak and the ways that He shouldn't speak. It is none of our business how God chooses to speak. We just need to be open to hear whichever way His communication flows to us.

Being a bilingual person, I have the ability to fluently speak English and Spanish. I once was engaged in a conversation and was speaking in Spanish when I overheard someone comment, "Speak English." Even though the person was just kidding, I immediately had a sense of my rights being violated. How dare that person think that he had the right to tell me which language I could or could not speak! While I forgave the jester, I used it as an opportunity to "educate" this person about individual's rights to speak in whichever language they preferred in their own private conversations.

With the same audacity, believers will usually tell God which language is approved for Him to speak to them. We want Him to speak in a way that makes us comfortable and that is on our level. On the contrary, God will talk to us on our level because He loves us, but He expects us to come up to His level and learn His ways.

The main reason some will try to control which method God uses to speak to them is because they'll claim that they have been more successful at hearing from God in one specific way over the others. That one specific way then becomes their "official" way to hear from God, and they will reject the other ways He speaks. As a result, you have believers who say that God talks to them *only* in Scriptures. Others will say God talks to them *only* in dreams, etc, etc.

The Holy Spirit is challenging us today to mature quickly. In the days in which we are living, we must come up to God's level and operate by the rules that He has established in His holy word. He wants to speak – let Him. If you have been guilty of putting God into a box with a laced ribbon, then repent for it and let Him out. You won't regret it!

Just as one person cannot know all of God, neither can I write this book and pretend to know all of the ways that God will use to communicate. In this chapter, I would like to look at other possible options that God would use to communicate to His children.

Nature

> "The heavens declare the glory of God;
> And the firmament shows His handiwork." Psalms 19:1

God will speak to you through nature. When you need to hear from the Lord, go out and enjoy the outdoors. Walk in the park, stroll over a bridge, or place a chair and sit at the beach. Let all of the smells, sounds and sights of the outdoors inspire you to give glory to God. By enjoying the creation, we are praising the One who created it.

Make sure to keep an open mind and spirit when you are out enjoying nature as God will speak to your heart while you take in its beauty. There's something about observing the creation that puts us at peace. We are forced to look at the handiwork of a Creator who loves His creation. We are also His handiwork and should realize that we are also an expression of His creativity and that He looks at us as an artist looks at his most prized work. He loves us for who we are – His creation!

Numbers

I want you to resist all of your desire to immediately assign the area of communication through numbers to the realm of the demonic. We have all seen the television advertisements that invite us to call Numerologists who will give us our "lucky" numbers. These psychics advertise that they can help you win the Lottery by playing the numbers that they give you.

Well, that is the counterfeit. Who created numbers anyway? There is only one Creator in the vast Universe – Jehovah, The Lord God Almighty. Our God is the God of all wisdom and knowledge and has provided for us what we would need to live a life on earth. God created numbers. Think about it, as early as the days of creation, the Bible is clear that there were numbers assigned to the days. For on day one God did one thing, on day two another, etc. On day seven, God rested. While there are different theories as to the length of each day, it is clear that numbers were assigned to the days for our convenience and understanding.

Since God created numbers, why wouldn't He be able to use them for His purposes? He can and certainly does. While there are no Bible chapters and verses that tell us specifically what each number symbolically represents, we must do a search within the

Bible to see how God uses certain numbers and how He assigns their meaning. Once that symbolism is revealed to you, you are now aware of how God may use that number to talk to you.

Here is a list of numbers and what they represent due to the context they were used in the Bible or in every day life.

1:                    Unity; the beginning of something.

2:                    Something established: confirmation.

3:                    God is in the matter; revelation.

4:                    Learning experience; you're about to encounter lessons.

5:                    Word of the Lord; expect to hear from Him.

6:                    The flesh.

7:                    Completion; perfection; full maturity.

8:                    New beginnings; covenant.

9:                    Holy Spirit; look to move in the gifts or walk in the fruit.

10:                   Set apart for a holy purpose.

11:                   Transition; filling the lack.

12:                   Leadership.

14:                   Double-grace!

30:                   Season to step into ministry.

33:                   Crucifying the flesh to live a resurrected life.

40:                   A season of testing.

50:                     Jubilee.

123:                    A series of events that will take place.

321:                    A countdown to an event.

These are just some examples of numbers and their possible meaning according to the context in which they were used. Now that you are aware of some possible meanings of numbers, God can begin to use your digital clock to minister to you.

Don't be surprised when you wake up at 3:33 a.m. Remember 3 is the number that shows up when God is involved in a matter. He will let you know that He is waking you up to spend time with you. Also, Jeremiah 33:3 says, *"Call to me and I will answer you, and show you great and mighty things, which you do not know."* Waking up at that time may be God's way of inviting you to receive revelation from Him.

If you wake up at 4:44 a.m., God may be alerting you as to a learning experience that you're about to walk through.

5:55 a.m. may signal to you that God has a rhema word for you. Get up and seek Him to receive what He has for you.

Activate yourself to hear from Him this way. When God sees that you're aware of this method of communication, He'll use it more to speak to you.

Rocks

Another interesting method that God uses is that He may speak to you through "rocks". What I basically mean by rocks is the people who do not serve the Lord. Actually, these may even mean people who are ungodly. Yet at a given moment, unbeknownst to them, they may be used as an oracle of the Lord to speak something to you as a message from the Lord. God will speak even through the rocks.

Children

Don't discount something that was spoken to you through smaller children. Whether they are your children or someone else's, they may be used by God to speak a word to you. I'm sure that all parents have had at least one encounter in which God has spoken something to us through our kids. Allow God to even use your own kids as messengers in your life.

Any Other Way He Chooses

Let God speak in whatever way He sees fit. If He speaks to you through a national event, say "Amen". If He communicates to you through the message of a movie, so be it. If He sends His words to you through an angel, receive it from the Lord.

One Piece of the Puzzle

An Anointed Detective is always on the hunt for more clues. Now as detectives, we are careful and do not take a clue and try to solve the case with only one piece of the puzzle. We must continue to prod and search to find other clues that confirm the evidence that we have already found.

Never let one piece of the puzzle cause you to make a major move in your life. Even if it is a vivid piece of revelation, always ask God to send you a confirmation, and He will.

Section III:

Organizing the Revelation

(Doing a Detective's Work.)

- 15 -
Consolidating the Revelation

By now, you have read about God's nature as a Communicator. You have also taken a step-by-step study into the various methods that God uses to communicate. I would like to congratulate you on getting this far in the book and encourage you to go all the way. Not only to read the entire book, but to begin to activate your detective's anointing.

Now that we have you activated to hear the voice of God, you are going to start hearing from heaven at a greater frequency than you've ever known. What do you do with all of that revelation?

Talking from experience, it is easy to quickly get overwhelmed. There were times when I felt so frustrated and defeated because I had a journal full of heavenly revelation, but had no idea what to do with any of it.

In this section, we are going to deal with what needs to be done after the revelation from God has been received. Oh yeah, the process is not done after you hear from God…it's only begun. The next few steps in this process is so crucial that if you overlook them, it would make all your efforts to hear from God meaningless.

You've Got to Record what You Receive

Okay, if you are not recording what you receive, you have just wasted your time and, most importantly, God's time. We are human beings, and we can tend to be very forgetful. You have to determine now which method you will use to track your communication from God.

In an earlier chapter, I covered some options. They were:

Journal:Using a journal book to write down what you see.

Tape Recorder:Using a recorder to capture your revelations.

Other: Any other creative way you can journal.

(For those of you who choose to use the tape recorder, be aware that tapes tend to mangle at times and may leave you tape-less.)

Here are some tips for those of you who choose to use the journal notebook method:

1 – Number and date your journals. This helps when you archive your journals so that you could shelf them in order. So your first journal could read, "Journal #1; January 1 – June 30, (Year)." Then your next one could read, "Journal #2, July 1 – December 31, (Year)." As you complete a new journal, you can now place them on a shelf or in a drawer in numerical sequence. This is helpful when you have to go back and dig out a piece of revelation that you have received prior.

2 – Find a method that works for you. You must find a method of journaling that will go with your lifestyle. Just make sure that your method will allow you to journal daily, journal while the revelation is still fresh and allows you to review the revelation regularly.

Now that you are recording and hearing from God, let's look at the next major step in consolidating revelation.

Consolidating the Pieces

Up to this point, you have heard from God and collected and journaled the puzzle pieces. Now you must take the final step of sitting down with all of those pieces and see if they fit.

Picture this: You need to make a decision for your life. You ask God in prayer to direct you. You have been watching carefully as an Anointed Detective, and you have received a few of the puzzle pieces. You have journaled what you've received. What do you do now? We are now looking at the final part of this process – bringing it all together.

As you review your journal, you must extract the pieces of revelation that God has sent to you about the decision you have to make. Now that you have all of those pieces before you, you must see if they fit to bring forth a perfect puzzle. Remember, when God sends you pieces of a puzzle, they all fit neatly together revealing His perfect will. This stage of the process requires some work on your part.

Start from the beginning: Organize the pieces by date

Here is why dating all the pieces of revelation is so helpful. Now that you are assembling all of the pieces of revelation from God, you're going to want to start at the beginning. What was that first piece that you received from God? When did He start talking to you about a matter? Pull that piece out and then keep digging out the other pieces that followed right up until your final piece. Place them in order by date and rehearse the matter from the beginning.

After you prayed, what piece did you get first? Then what happened after that? You catch the drift? Force yourself to look at your life from when you prayed and asked for God's help, to when the answer arrived.

Let's make our example more definite. Let's say that you were asking God to show you if you should go on a vacation or not. After your prayer, you journaled four puzzle pieces that you believe were directed at answering your question about this vacation. You now have to go through your journal and extract all the pieces that you believe fit this puzzle. So let's get our four example pieces.

Piece #1 – (Scripture) After your prayer, you felt that Psalms 37:4 was quickened to you. *"Delight yourself also in the Lord, and He shall give you the desires of your heart."*

But…you know that you cannot make a life decision on only 1 piece of revelation. You don't want to be deceived by your own desires. So you ask God to send you more pieces.

Piece #2 – (Dream) You had a dream in which you stood before a travel agent and they said to you that your travel tickets were ready to be picked up. After prayer, your interpretation was that now was the time to get the tickets.

You know that "out of the mouth of 2 or 3 witnesses shall every word be established." So, you're okay with these two pieces and decide to see if your circumstances line up and confirm your revelation.

Piece #3 – (People) Without you mentioning a word to anyone, the next day more than a few people have mentioned to you that you should go on a vacation. You know that it's no coincidence but a God event, so you journal this piece too.

Piece #4 – (Circumstances) When you ask your boss for the time off, he said that it was okay. When you called your travel agent, they not only had availabilities, but you received a special discount.

RESULT – You go on vacation and have a wonderful time. Everything worked out beautifully because as you sought the hand of the Lord, He directed you every step of the way. Once God opened the door for you to go on vacation, you can trust that everything will work out fine including the weather, the prices, the accommodations, and God will even work out divine connections with people He wants you to meet.

There you have an example of how an Anointed Detective listens to the voice of God, then works on assembling the pieces to know what God is saying. In the above example, I'm sure that even if God had blocked you from going on vacation, it would have been for your benefit. Let's look at another example.

You are now asking God to speak to you about a job offer that you have received. You're wondering if you should accept it. After pressing in to the Lord, you begin to function as an Anointed Detective looking for His clues. After a few days, you receive three pieces that speak to you regarding this decision. You sit down and pull the three pieces out and see if they fit.

Piece #1 – (Opportunity) Without you looking for a job, someone made you a job offer. The salary is a little higher and would meet your current needs. The spontaneity of it made you wonder if God was in it. Therefore, you journaled this piece.

Piece #2 – (Spirit) As you praying about this job offer, you notice that you have an unsettling feeling in your spirit. You don't feel at piece about taking it. You like your current job and as you think about leaving, you feel more ruffled in the spirit. It's enough to get your attention, and you journal it.

Piece #3 – (Circumstance) As you decide to test out the circumstance of the lack of peace you feel about leaving your current employment, you meet with your employer to let them know that you've been offered a job. They don't want to lose you and offer you a salary increment to match that of the offer.

RESULT – You kindly decline the new job offer, and you stay with your current employer. You have received the "two or three witnesses" that helped you determine the voice of God through this decision making process. The result is also that you now know that you are exactly where God wants you. Praise God!

You may wonder, "Well, what would have happened if they got different clues that contradicted each other? What if one clue said 'Take the job!' and the other clue said, 'Don't take the job?'" That is a good question. Being that we are humans, as we are looking to hear from God, we'll have to battle our thoughts and our own heart's desires. Many times it is the voice of the heart that is speaking, hoping beyond all that it's desires will be fulfilled. So, what advice would I give the person who is having contradictory revelation? Don't move!

Remember, when God speaks to you, all the pieces will line up. If the pieces are contradicting each other, then you cannot build a case that God has spoken, because when He does, everything meshes beautifully. That's how He works. Contradictory pieces of revelation are a sign that it is not God.

Good News for the Gentiles

Let's look at another example. This time, let's read about an Anointed Detective from the Scriptures who picked up on God's puzzle pieces – the Apostle Peter.

After Jesus' death and resurrection, God established a new covenant with not only the Jews, but the gentiles as well. Before, any gentile who wanted to serve the Lord God Almighty would have to become a proselyte. They would have to convert and submit themselves entirely to the law. Now, salvation was made available for any man who would believe in Jesus as the Son of God and receive His sacrifice for their sins. Talk about a major paradigm shift!

While this was a new covenant that God established, He was just about to inform His children on earth about it.

> "There was a certain man in Caesarea called Cornelius, a centurion of what was called the Italian Regiment, a devout man and one who feared God with all his household, who gave alms generously to the people, and prayed to God always. About the ninth hour of the day he saw clearly in a vision an angel of God coming in and saying to him, 'Cornelius!' And when he observed him, he was afraid, and said, 'What is it, lord?' So he said to him, 'Your prayers and your alms have come up for a memorial before God. **Now send men to Joppa, and send for Simon whose surname is Peter. He is lodging with Simon, a tanner, whose house is by the sea. He will tell you what you must do.'** And when the angel who spoke to him had departed, Cornelius called two of his household servants and a devout soldier from among those who waited on him continually. So when he had explained all these things to them, he sent them to Joppa." Acts 10:1-8 emphasis mine

Cornelius was an upright gentile; gentile meaning he was not Jewish. He received a revelation from heaven telling him to send for Peter. With this initial visitation that Cornelius received, God set the plan in motion to reveal this new covenant. For our sakes...let's start

to journal the pieces that God was sending about this new revelation.
***Puzzle Piece #1 – (Angel) Cornelius the gentile receives a visit
from an angel telling him to send for Peter.***

> "The next day, as they went on their journey and drew near the
> city, Peter went up on the housetop to pray, about the sixth hour.
> Then he became very hungry and wanted to eat; **but while they
> made ready, he fell into a trance** and saw heaven opened and
> an object like a great sheet bound at the four corners,
> descending to him and let down to the earth. In it were all kinds
> of four-footed animals of the earth, wild beasts, creeping things,
> and birds of the air. And a voice came to him, 'Rise, Peter; kill
> and eat.' But Peter said, 'Not so, Lord! For I have never eaten
> anything common or unclean.' And a voice spoke to him again
> the second time, 'What God has cleansed you must not call
> common.' **This was done three times.** And the object was
> taken up into heaven again." Acts 10:9-16 (emphasis mine)

***Puzzle Piece #2 – (Trance) It was revealed to Peter in a trance
not to call common what God has cleansed.*** *(God was preparing
Peter to go into a gentile's (Cornelius) home to present the gospel.
Jews believed that gentiles were unclean and would normally not
enter their homes.)*

***Puzzle Piece #3 – (Numbers) The vision was repeated 3 times.
Remember, 3 is a number that God uses to confirm that He is
involved in a matter.***

> *"Now while Peter wondered within himself what this vision which
> he had seen meant, behold, the men who had been sent from
> Cornelius had made inquiry for Simon's house, and stood before
> the gate. And they called and asked whether Simon, whose
> surname was Peter, was lodging there. **While Peter thought
> about the vision, the Spirit said to him, 'Behold, three men
> are seeking you. Arise therefore, go down and go with
> them, doubting nothing; for I have sent them.'** Then Peter
> went down to the men who had been sent to him from Cornelius,
> and said, 'Yes, I am he whom you seek. For what reason have
> you come?' And they said, 'Cornelius the centurion, a just man,
> one who fears God and has a good reputation among all the
> nation of the Jews, was divinely instructed by a holy angel to
> summon you to his house, and to hear words from you.' Then he*

invited them in and lodged them. On the next day Peter went away with them, and some brethren from Joppa accompanied him." Acts 10:17-23 (emphasis mine)

Puzzle Piece #4 – (Voice of the Holy Spirit) While Peter pondered on the meaning of the trance, the Holy Spirit spoke to him that three men would be looking for him. Peter was to go with them without doubting anything.

Puzzle Piece #5 – (Circumstances) Three men actually showed up looking for Peter.

Puzzle Piece #6 – (Numbers) How many men came to get Peter? There's that number 3 again. God is proving that He is in the matter.

"And the following day they entered Caesarea. Now Cornelius was waiting for them, and had called together his relatives and close friends. As Peter was coming in, Cornelius met him and fell down at his feet and worshiped him. But Peter lifted him up, saying, 'Stand up; I myself am also a man.' And as he talked with him, he went in and found many who had come together. Then he said to them, 'You know how unlawful it is for a Jewish man to keep company with or go to one of another nation. But God has shown me that I should not call any man common or unclean. Therefore I came without objection as soon as I was sent for. I ask, then, for what reason have you sent for me?' So Cornelius said, 'Four days ago I was fasting until this hour; and at the ninth hour I prayed in my house, and behold, a man stood before me in bright clothing, and said: Cornelius, your prayer has been heard, and your alms are remembered in the sight of God. Send therefore to Joppa and call Simon here, whose surname is Peter. He is lodging in the house of Simon, a tanner, by the sea. When he comes, he will speak to you. So I sent to you immediately, and you have done well to come. Now therefore, we are all present before God, to hear all the things commanded you by God.'" Acts 10:24-33

In this segment of the Scriptures we see that all of the puzzle pieces are falling into place beautifully. Peter is following through with his revelation, and he finds himself in the home of a gentile who has his whole family gathered to hear whatever news Peter brings.

Notice that when Peter asks Cornelius the purpose of this visit, Cornelius **rehearses** the matter from the beginning. He starts with puzzle piece #1 and explains to Peter why he sent for him. Now, bear in mind that up to this point, Peter and Cornelius are both still in the dark as to why God wanted them to meet. Let's keep reading.

> *"Then Peter opened his mouth and said: In truth I perceive that God shows no partiality. But in every nation whoever fears Him and works righteousness is accepted by Him. The word which God sent to the children of Israel, preaching peace through Jesus Christ—He is Lord of all— that word you know, which was proclaimed throughout all Judea, and began from Galilee after the baptism which John preached: how God anointed Jesus of Nazareth with the Holy Spirit and with power, who went about doing good and healing all who were oppressed by the devil, for God was with Him. And we are witnesses of all things which He did both in the land of the Jews and in Jerusalem, whom they killed by hanging on a tree. Him God raised up on the third day, and showed Him openly, not to all the people, but to witnesses chosen before by God, even to us who ate and drank with Him after He arose from the dead. And He commanded us to preach to the people, and to testify that it is He who was ordained by God to be Judge of the living and the dead. To Him all the prophets witness that, through His name, whoever believes in Him will receive remission of sins." Acts 10:34-43*

God gives Peter the opportunity to preach the gospel to a houseful of gentiles. How cool is that!

> *"**While Peter was still speaking these words, the Holy Spirit fell upon all those who heard the word. And those of the circumcision who believed were astonished, as many as came with Peter, because the gift of the Holy Spirit had been poured out on the Gentiles also. For they heard them speak with tongues and magnify God.** Then Peter answered, 'Can anyone forbid water, that these should not be baptized who have received the Holy Spirit just as we have?' And he commanded them to be baptized in the name of the Lord. Then they asked him to stay a few days." Acts 10:44-48 (emphasis mine)*

Puzzle Piece #7 – (Prophetic Event) As Peter was preaching, the Holy Spirit fell upon those who were listening, and they

received the gift of the Holy Spirit of speaking in tongues. God
had filled the gentiles just as He did those gathered on the day
of Pentecost (Acts 2). Through this event, God was speaking
that He was also pouring His Spirit over the gentiles and they
were now able to receive salvation through Jesus Christ.

Peter was instrumental in the new move God was doing to
include the gentiles. Although he was used by God, he was about to
be faced with some opposition.

> *"Now the apostles and brethren who were in Judea heard that the*
> *Gentiles had also received the word of God. And when Peter*
> *came up to Jerusalem, those of the circumcision contended with*
> *him, saying, 'You went in to uncircumcised men and ate with*
> *them!' Acts 11:1-3*

Ooh, Peter was in trouble! Or was he? Word had spread
quickly what had occurred in Cornelius' house. They were waiting for
Peter to get home so they could pounce on him. The Bible says that
they "contended" with him. They must have thought that 'ole Peter
had lost his mind. He knew better than to enter the house of a
gentile. What was wrong with him? They were going to set him
straight. Let's look at Peter's response.

> "But Peter explained it to them in order from the beginning,
> saying…" Acts 11:4 (emphasis mine)

Do you see how Peter substantiated what occurred? He "explained it to them in order from the beginning." When you are reviewing your puzzle pieces from God, it is essential that you review it
from the beginning. When did God start talking to you, and how did
the revelation play out? Those are questions that you must be able
to ponder and answer clearly.

> *"But Peter explained it to them in order from the beginning,*
> *saying, 'I was in the city of Joppa praying; **and in a trance I saw***
> ***a vision**, an object descending like a great sheet, let down from*
> *heaven by four corners; and it came to me. When I observed it*
> *intently and considered, I saw four-footed animals of the earth,*
> *wild beasts, creeping things, and birds of the air. **And I heard a***
> ***voice** saying to me, 'Rise, Peter; kill and eat.' But I said, 'Not*
> *so, Lord! For nothing common or unclean has at any time entered*

*my mouth.' But the voice answered me again from heaven,
'What God has cleansed you must not call common.'* **Now this
was done three times, and all were drawn up again into heaven.**
At that very moment, **three men stood before the house where
I was, having been sent to me from Caesarea. Then the Spirit
told me to go with them, doubting nothing. Moreover these
six brethren accompanied me,** *and we entered the man's
house.* **And he told us how he had seen an angel standing in
his house,** *who said to him,* **'Send men to Joppa, and call for
Simon whose surname is Peter,** *who will tell you words by which
you and all your household will be saved.'* **And as I began to
speak, the Holy Spirit fell upon them, as upon us at the
beginning. Then I remembered the word of the Lord, how
He said, 'John indeed baptized with water, but you shall be
baptized with the Holy Spirit.'** *If therefore God gave them the
same gift as He gave us when we believed on the Lord Jesus
Christ, who was I that I could withstand God?'* **When they heard
these things they became silent; and they glorified God,
saying, 'Then God has also granted to the Gentiles
repentance to life.'"** Acts 11:4-18 (emphasis mine)

Peter rehearsed the matter from the beginning. Apart from the
already mentioned puzzle pieces, Peter includes two more pieces:

#1 – Six brethren accompanied him. Peter was the seventh to
those six, which means, completion. With every step that Peter took
towards Cornelius' house with those six men, God was prophesying
that He was fulfilling the new covenant that He had planned from the
beginning.

#2 – Then Peter said he "remembered" (God-thought) the words
of the Lord who said that "John baptized with water, but you shall be
baptized with the Holy Spirit."

RESULT – The end result was the confession of those who had
heard Peter: "God had indeed granted repentance to life to the
gentiles."

Do you see how through this whole process, God had to walk
Peter step-by-step giving him just enough information for the next
step? Notice that God didn't tell Peter at the beginning what He was
planning on doing. He only gave Peter 1 piece of the puzzle. Peter

had to take that one piece and follow it to the next piece, trusting in God's guidance.

This is how it works! God will give us 1 piece of the puzzle and will expect us to walk and trust that He will guide us as we look for the next step we're to take.

My Call to Full-Time Ministry

When I was in the work force, I was a Program Director at a Faith-Based-Organization. While I was grateful that it provided a living for my family, I longed for the day when I could do ministry full-time. I always thought that if God called me into the ministry full-time, He would do it when I was debt-free and had money saved up so that money wouldn't be an issue.

The program I had overseen had secured a five-year grant from the State of New York to operate. Two years into that contract, God began to speak to me about a shift.

One morning as I was waking up from my dream, I heard a voice say to me, "When it was time for Elijah to move on, I dried the brook." (Puzzle Piece #1) I had absolutely no idea what that meant and why God was saying that to me. I went into work later that day and to my surprise, I found a letter from our funders at New York State informing us that our grant would be ending in 3 months. Even though we still had 3 years left of grant funding, we were being cut early. (Puzzle Piece #2)

Immediately, I began to pray and to press in asking God to show me what I was to do next. After spending time in prayer early one morning, I returned to my bed to catch some sleep. As soon as I closed my eyes, I had a vivid dream that lasted about 5 minutes. Here is the dream:

> *My wife and I are in a beautiful red sports car driving on a highway in a desert. The background looked as if we were driving through Nevada's arid landscape. The car was driving fast! Even though I could steer the car, I had no control over its speed. Suddenly, I noticed that there was a ramp coming up with a fork in the highway. Above the fork I saw a sign that had two*

arrows: one pointing to the left and one to the right. We were approaching the fork quickly, and I yelled out at my wife, "Honey, which way are we going?" She wouldn't respond. So I yelled louder, "Which way are we going? If we go right, where will that take us? What about if we go left?" To no avail, it was as if my wife couldn't hear me. Before I knew it, we were at the fork in the road. Just as we were going to run into the sign, my instincts took over, and I yanked the steering wheel to the right and continued driving. Then I woke up.

As I woke up from that dream, my heart was racing. I instantly knew what God was telling me. He was telling me that the car represented my ministry. That God had placed us on a fast track and that we were quickly approaching a decision (fork) that we had to make. The Nevada landscape spoke to me of this dry area of my life where I needed to know what God wanted me to do. My wife not speaking to me showed me that this direction would not come from brainstorming with family but from Him. Just as I tried to process which direction to go, God was letting me know that in the natural I would want more time to analyze my decision, but I would not have it; I would have to trust and obey. As I approached the sign, my instincts took over and I veered to the right. The Lord was showing me to trust my faith in Him that He would veer us in the "right" direction. I was to trust that God was guiding me. (Puzzle Piece #3)

Just before my job was to finish, I had another dream.

In this dream, I was at the unemployment office. As I approached the clerk in the window, she asked for my name. I responded, "Hector Santos." She got very excited and said, "Hector Santos? We were just briefed on your case this morning. What an honor to meet you." I was shocked at her response to me. She then said, "We were all informed to tell you that yes, we will help you until you find your next grant." I was so excited to hear this news. She then asked for my identification, which I was trying to locate fumbling through my wallet. Then I woke up.

After working on this dream to get the interpretation, here is what I received from the Lord. "I want you to go to the unemployment office. They will help you with the next step." (Puzzle Piece #4)

Now, I have to admit, I had a real hard time with that command. Being a college graduate, I was pained at the thought of having to be on unemployment. It was just something that went against my grain. Nonetheless, I applied and began to receive my unemployment benefits.

Shortly afterwards, I received a letter from unemployment telling me that I was being invited to hear about a new program that they were starting. So, out of curiosity, I attended this orientation.

When anyone is on unemployment, their full focus has to go towards finding other employment. If the Department of Labor ever found out that someone was starting a business while on unemployment, it could result in the immediate elimination of benefits, and there might be a suit brought against the person. The gist of this whole new program was that it offered select individuals that met a certain criteria another option. Rather than look for a job, you could use your weekly benefit to start a business under the Department of Labor's supervision.

As I sat there listening to the presentation, I felt it was a waste of time because I didn't have a business to start-up. There were people there who were looking to start landscape businesses, beauty parlors, etc. As I was exiting the room, I was asked if I would apply to the program. I told the gentleman, "Well, I don't really have a business. I am looking more to enter the ministry." He answered, "Are you an Ordained Minister?" "Yes," I replied. "Well then, just apply and see what they tell you. The worst they could say is no."

I applied for the program and was surprised to find out 3 weeks later that I was accepted. So rather than have to look for a new job, I had to work full-time to start my ministry. I had to agree to take 20 hours of business training, meet with a business coach and send in weekly vouchers. In return, I would get my normal weekly benefit, which wouldn't be affected no matter how much money I would bring in from my business (ministry). The program was a God-send for me. (Puzzle Piece #5)

God in His wisdom opened up an opportunity for me to not only receive start-up funding for the ministry, but also have the training necessary to establish a ministry.

These 5 puzzle pieces were what gave me the knowing that God was calling me to the full-time ministry. I have since continued to work for the Kingdom of God, and I'm loving every minute of it.

Recap

So, let's go over the process of consolidating revelation one more time. When you are seeking God for an answer to your prayer:

1 – Look for Him to respond.

2 – Journal His response.

3 – When you've received several puzzle pieces, sit down and organize them in order by date.

4 – As you're going over them, rehearse the matter from the beginning.

5 – Look to see if the pieces fit well and what the response is.

6 – Receive the instruction from the Lord.

7 – Obey what the Lord has given you.

The more you practice consolidating revelation, the better you will get at it. Determine from the outset that you are going to develop the skill to do this. Don't allow yourself to get discouraged. Hang in there and allow God to be your help. In no time, you'll realize that it becomes like second nature.

Monday Jan. 13	OFFICES CLOSED
Tuesday Jan. 14	Overseers meeting @ 6:30 pm *Happy Birthday Durene Lamoree*
Wednesday Jan. 15	COFFEE TALK – Noon to 1 pm Bible Study - 6 pm – Studying Revelation Peaks, Pits, Praises, Prayer - 7 pm *Happy Birthday Melissa Terry*
Thursday Jan. 16	Bible Study – Meet @ 7 pm to go across street *"Through the Bible"* Godly Women's Fellowship (Ages 18-35) & Bible Study in Conference Room – 7 pm
Friday Jan. 17	AMPLIFY YOUTH GROUP 6:30-8:30 pm
Saturday Jan. 18	*Happy Birthday Judy Osborne*
Sunday Jan. 19	**8:30 am Service** **10:15 am Sunday School** Adult "Higher Ground" Discipleship Class meets in Fellowship Hall with snacks & refreshments Discipleship Class #3 10:15 in Conference Room with Pastor Dann All other classes in classrooms **11:15 am Service** Gatewatcher Tony Nard

Baby Crying Room
ilable during service
in the rear of the
Sanctuary

cipleship Classes:
ges: Newborn - 4
5-7
8-12
Teen
Adult

hildren's Church
ring 2nd service
school 4 & under
Ages 5-7
8-12

WINTER

Drawn to Jesus

Humble yourselves therefore
under the mighty hand of God,
so that He may exalt you in due
time, casting all your care
upon Him, because He
cares about you. -1 Peter 5:6-7

Supplies Nashville, TN.

BROADMAN
CHURCH SUPPLIES

Scripture from HCSB®
081407003450

Crossroads of Life Church

Vision Statement: *"Let God Arise"*

Pastor—Rev. Dann E. Travis, revdann@verizon.net
Assistant Pastor—Rev. Brian Lalli, revbrian@verizon.net
20 Exchange St., Binghamton, NY 13901
607-724-6383
Office: debrand1@verizon.net
Website: www.crossroadsoflifechurch.com
www.facebook.com/CrossroadsofLifeChurch

Like us?
👍 **Like us!**

January 5, 2013

WELCOME GUESTS!

Please be sure to get a guest packet, fill out the information and put it in the offering plate. We'd like to get to know you.

<u>Discipleship Class #2</u>
Starts today in the Conference Room with Pastor Dann during Sunday School

What is...
Christian Discipleship?

Pastor Dann's sermons are televised every Monday night @ 9:30 pm on TW cable channel 4

*DVD's - $5 CD's - $2
Order copies at Hospitality Table

Join us @ 10:15 am
in the Fellowship Hall
for Adult Discipleship
Includes snacks & refreshments

Christian Radio & Web Sites for our area:
Family Life Network: 88.5 on the radio, www.fln.org
Montrose Radio: 96.5 fm, 800 am,, www.wpel.org
Christian Broadcasting Network: www.cbn.com
Today's Christian Music Magazine: www.todayschristianmusic.com
Christian Satellite Network: 104.9, http://www.csnradio.com

Our Bi-Annual Business Meeting will be held on January
7 pm. Snow date is January 28th.
Please see the display in the front foyer for the by-law ch
be voted on at the meeting.
We will also have elections and a special presentatio
members are encouraged to attend.

"Psychologists tell us that January is the most depressing
year. One expert has specifically postulated that January
most depressing day of the year. What happened to our fr
all the excitement of new resolve?"

At one of the great low points of his life, King David fo
exiled in the desert after the betrayal of his son Absalom.
his loyal followers, exiled from all of his possessions, st
regal position, and estranged from his family and friends
down overwhelming disappointments. In this mome
recalibration he wrote, "My soul, wait silently for God
expectation is from Him. He only is my rock and my sa
my defense; I shall not be moved. In God is my salvatio
the rock of my strength, and my refuge, is in God. Trus
times, you people; Pour out your heart before Him; God
us" (Psalm 62:5-8).

After struggling with superficial measurements a
comparisons, another Psalmist learned that the ultimat
placing our desires and hopes in the power and pleasur
of God (Psalm 73:18). He prayed, "Whom have I in h
And there is none upon earth that I desire besides Yo
my heart fail; But God is the strength of my heart a
forever" (vv. 25-26).

The lesson seems to be that we should hold our expect
place our faith and hope firmly in the reliable faithful
of God. Sometimes our celebrations and resolution
and satisfying. Sometimes they fail to deliver. In it
Christ, not circumstances, to meet our needs. One
way: "Keep high aspirations, moderate expectations.

Through the seasons of life we are wise to realize
understands and provides abundant grace fo
disappointments. Only Christ is sufficient for
expectations, and needs. Truly, Jesus ne
Copyright © 2014 Daniel Henderson. All ri

- 16 -
Welcome to the Army of Anointed Detectives

Now the Real Training Begins

I remember when I was studying to get my driver's license. I read the book backward and forward to make sure that I had all of the details just right. After taking the written exam, I was thrilled to see that I scored 100% on the test. I didn't know, however, that while I had the book knowledge of being a driver, I also needed hands-on experience.

Thinking I was a professional, I climbed behind the wheel of the first car that I was going to practice on. My instructor told me to drive it slowly up an alley. I slowly drove the car in the direction I was told. It was frightening! All the rules in my head became like mush as I nervously learned how to drive forward, look in the side and rear view mirrors and avoid pot holes all at the same time.

Just as we were approaching the end, the instructor told me to park next to a parked car. As I moved the vehicle towards the parked car, my instructor told me to slow down. In my nervousness, I went to press on the brakes and accidentally put the gas pedal to the floor. Instantly, we were speeding towards the parked car. My instructor yelled, "Oh no, you're going to crash!" Suddenly, I quickly slammed on the brake as our bodies jolted forward. I looked up to survey the damage and realized that we had come about half and inch from the parked car. As I looked over to my instructor, I saw him sitting there frozen with his hands over his eyes. "You can look now," I said to him. He slowly removed his hands and let out a sigh when he realized that the accident had been averted.

I'll never forget that driving lesson. I learned that head knowledge is so much more effective when it goes hand in hand with experience. Why am I saying this to you? Don't look to load up on all the head knowledge for knowledge's sake. Get the knowledge, but also start walking it out and get the experience as well. When you get the experience to help you understand your knowledge, that's when you really digest the information, and it becomes personal to you.

Do you realize that even though we take a driver's test to get our license, it is not at that point when we learn how to drive? We take driving lessons to prepare for the driving test. It is usually after we get our license, however, that we perfect our skills as drivers. I've been on the road for numerous years and over that time I have become a much better driver. As a matter of fact, I can even spot new drivers by the way they drive.

This book is designed to give you the information and the encouragement to start stepping into the flow. Just like the student driver, you will have your instructor, the Holy Spirit, ease you onto the highway of revelation. Slowly but surely you will make your way into a new realm of hearing communication from the True and Living God. While this is great news, this is not the part where you become mature in your hearing from heaven. It is after you get started initially and you make your commitment to hear from heaven on a daily basis. It is over the process of time when you will flourish and develop a pure gift from God.

Maybe after time you'll notice those who are newer in the dimension of the Spirit. Do we laugh at them and point out their immaturity? Absolutely not! We will encourage them also to join the army of Anointed Detectives who hear the voice of God and serve as mentors to help them grow quickly in understanding the things of the Spirit.

Now that you have some head knowledge, the true training begins. Day in and day out, the Holy Spirit will respond to the cry of your heart to hear from heaven. He will walk with you, lead you, inspire you, communicate to you and train you on how to be an Anointed Detective.

Submit yourself to the training and do not back out. The dropout rate may be high, but for those who see the training through, they will enjoy a level of life that is unparalleled.

~ They will enjoy intimacy with the Father.

~ They will always be steps ahead of the enemy.

~ They will be led into all truth.

~ They will always be at the right place at the right time.

~ They will have a fountain of communication flowing through them to   others. This is where the gifts of the Spirit are really unleashed.

~ They will be in the perfect will of God.

~ They will bear much fruit for the Kingdom of God.

Do you see that the benefits outweigh the risks? It is so worth entering the army of Anointed Detectives.

We are Needed to Shine

We are living in a world that is dying. People are starving to know that there is a God and that He knows them personally and intimately. The devil understands this and has unleashed his campaign to promote his counterfeit communication. If he can supply his deadly communication and meet the demand that is coming from this spiritual hunger, he will do so. He will even attempt to reach souls for his kingdom before the Kingdom of God.

The devil's army is trained and mobilized. They are ready. His psychics, fortune-tellers, cult leaders, mediums, witches, warlocks, new agers, Satanists and all others are already doing their recruitment. They are out spreading their message that they can tell you your future, that they can give you direction for your life, and that they know the purpose for your life. The sad thing is that they are being successful at deceiving a multitude of God's children. As they deceive the masses, they are using our God-given methods. They have taken hold of dreams, visions, trances, etc. for the kingdom of darkness. What should we do?

This is our time to rise up! We must stand up firm and strong and begin to function the way our heavenly Father created us – as revelatory beings. Let's develop our senses to hear from heaven. Let's make hearing the voice of God a high priority in our lives. Nothing else is as important as being open before His voice.

I believe the day will come when the world will know that they have prophets and prophetic believers in their midst. The police shouldn't run to psychics to find out where missing people are or who robbed the bank. The day will come when it will be God's true prophets and prophetic believers that are ready to bring God's insight forth to solve mysteries.

God needs us to shine His light into this dark world. They are out there praying for God to hear them and save them. We are their hope. Let's tune in to God and be His hands, feet and voice extended in this realm.

A Touched Soul

I once took a group out to do some prophetic evangelism. Basically, what this means is that we go on the street and prophesy to people and tell them about Jesus. On this occasion we went to a local college. As we walked the campus of the college, we prayed for a "woman at the well" experience. We continued to look around for a student that we could minister to. Even though it was a sunny Saturday morning, the campus seemed empty.

Deciding to change our strategy, I left two of my team behind to pray and intercede for a student while I took a young team member, Christine. Just as we approached the end of a hallway, we heard coins being deposited into a vending machine. As we rounded the corner, we found a young African-American gal getting food from the machines. We approached her.

"Hello, we're from a local church, and we're out in the neighborhood praying for people. Is it okay if we pray for you and tell you what God is saying to you?" I asked.

After a long pause of hesitation she replied, "Okay, go ahead." I prayed a quick prayer and then began to prophesy. "I hear the Lord saying that you have wanted to stand firm and remain pure. However, you have had some pressure coming against you..." When I said that, she interrupted me with a loud yell. "You're kidding me! You're kidding me, right?" she asked confused.

"What do you mean?" I replied.

"How do you know what's going on with me?" She asked as her eyes began to well up with tears.

"Well, we didn't know what's going on with you. As we pray, we listen to what God is saying and that is what He said to us about you."

"No! How do you know that?" She began to sob out loud, and I saw that her tears began to form a puddle at her feet. "How do you know that? Is this for real? Is this for real?" By this time I was getting concerned because she was shouting. I couldn't help but picture security rounding the corner and tossing us out of there.

"Why would God show you that about me? I don't understand," she commented.

"He showed us that because He loves you. He knows your heart, and He hears your prayers." I responded.

"You don't understand," she said. "I broke up with my boyfriend a while ago because he was a bad influence on me. I have been successful at keeping him away, and just today he called me trying to get together with me again. I finally gave in and told him that if he picked me up at school within the next 5 minutes that I would go with him. Just after hanging up the phone, I prayed, 'God, if I ever needed You to help me, I need You now.' That's about the time when you came up to me and asked me if you could pray. How did you know?"

"God told me." Just then, I forgot that I hadn't given her our names. So I said, "I'm sorry, I forgot to give you our names. I'm Hector and this is Christine." What's your name?"

"Sequoia," she replied.

Christine jumped up in complete amazement and said, "That's amazing. When I was praying for you, God kept showing me a picture of a Sequoia tree, and I didn't know why. Now I know. Just like a sequoia tree is firm and tall, God says that he wants to firm you in Him and help you grow in Him as well." Hearing this word left me amazed at how much God knew this girl and His plans for her life.

Sequoia began to sob and cry, and I finally had to convince her to have a seat. After talking to her some more and talking to her about Jesus, she said that she was not ready to make a commitment. It amazes me how God can be so clear with some people, and yet they don't make a move towards their Maker.

We left her with the information to visit our church when she was ready and with a promise to continue praying for her. Even though she didn't accept Jesus as her Savior, I knew that some powerful seeds were sown into her heart about God's reality and His love towards her.

Once you have activated yourself in hearing from God, He will use it not only in your life but in the lives of others as well.

A Clarion Call

I started this book telling you about a vision that the Lord showed me (when I was a child) about the nations that He would send me to in His name. The Lord continues to impress upon me the shortness of the time. We have to work diligently and quickly to do our part to expand the Kingdom of Heaven in our world. After all, Jesus did tell us to "occupy" until He returned. As time continues to quickly go by, the Lord continues to speak to me about raising up a prophetic army. In order to advance, we must be prophetic!

There is a clarion call going out in the realm of the Spirit. God is calling us to join the end-time prophetic army. He is looking for you to join this army and to be a channel in which He can flow. Will you respond?

For those who have taken a bold step forward, I say to you, "Welcome to the army of Anointed Detectives!"

WINTER

Drawn to Jesus

Humble yourselves therefore
under the mighty hand of God,
so that He may exalt you in due
time, casting all your care
upon Him, because He
cares about you. -1 Peter 5:6-7

Crossroads of Life Church

Vision Statement: *"Let God Arise"*

Pastor—Rev. Dann E. Travis, revdann@verizon.net
Assistant Pastor—Rev. Brian Lalli, revbrian@verizon.net
20 Exchange St., Binghamton, NY 13901
607-724-6383
Office: debrand1@verizon.net
Website: www.crossroadsoflifechurch.com
www.facebook.com/CrossroadsofLifeChurch

Like us?

January 5, 2013

WELCOME GUESTS! Please be sure to get a guest packet, fill out the information and put it in the offering plate. We'd like to get to know you.

Discipleship Class #2
Starts today in the Conference
Room with Pastor Dann
during Sunday School

What is...
Christian Discipleship?

Pastor Dann's sermons
are televised
every Monday night
@ 9:30 pm on
TW cable channel 4

*DVD's - $5 CD's - $2
Order copies at Hospitality Table

***Join us @ 10:15 am
in the Fellowship Hall
for Adult Discipleship***
*Includes snacks &
refreshments*

Christian Radio & Web Sites for our area:
Family Life Network: 88.5 on the radio, www.fln.org
Montrose Radio: 96.5 fm, 800 am,, www.wpel.org
Christian Broadcasting Network: www.cbn.com
Today's Christian Music Magazine: www.todayschristianmusic.com
Christian Satellite Network: 104.9, http://www.csnradio.com

Our Bi-Annual Business Meeting will be held on January 21st @ 7 pm. Snow date is January 28th.
Please see the display in the front foyer for the by-law changes to be voted on at the meeting.
We will also have elections and a special presentation. All members are encouraged to attend.

"Psychologists tell us that January is the most depressing month of the year. One expert has specifically postulated that January 18th is the most depressing day of the year. What happened to our fresh start and all the excitement of new resolve?"

At one of the great low points of his life, King David found himself exiled in the desert after the betrayal of his son Absalom. Forsaken by his loyal followers, exiled from all of his possessions, stripped of his regal position, and estranged from his family and friends, David faced down overwhelming disappointments. In this moment of soul recalibration he wrote, "My soul, wait silently for God alone, for my expectation is from Him. He only is my rock and my salvation; He is my defense; I shall not be moved. In God is my salvation and my glory; the rock of my strength, and my refuge, is in God. Trust in Him at all times, you people; Pour out your heart before Him; God is a refuge for us" (Psalm 62:5-8).

After struggling with superficial measurements and surface comparisons, another Psalmist learned that the ultimate good in life is placing our desires and hopes in the power and pleasure of the nearness of God (Psalm 73:18). He prayed, "Whom have I in heaven but You? And there is none upon earth that I desire besides You. My flesh and my heart fail; But God is the strength of my heart and my portion forever" (vv. 25-26).

The lesson seems to be that we should hold our expectations loosely, but place our faith and hope firmly in the reliable faithfulness and goodness of God. Sometimes our celebrations and resolutions are invigorating and satisfying. Sometimes they fail to deliver. In it all, we must trust Christ, not circumstances, to meet our needs. One advisor said it this way: "Keep high aspirations, moderate expectations, and small needs."

Through the seasons of life we are wise to realize that only the Lord understands and provides abundant grace for our deepest disappointments. Only Christ is sufficient for our aspirations, expectations, and needs. Truly, Jesus never fails.

Monday Jan. 13	OFFICES CLOSED
Tuesday Jan. 14	Overseers meeting @ 6:30 pm *Happy Birthday Durene Lamoree*
Wednesday Jan. 15	COFFEE TALK – Noon to 1 pm Bible Study - 6 pm – Studying Revelation Peaks, Pits, Praises, Prayer - 7 pm *Happy Birthday Melissa Terry*
Thursday Jan. 16	Bible Study – Meet @ 7 pm to go across street *"Through the Bible"* Godly Women's Fellowship (Ages 18-35) & Bible Study in Conference Room – 7 pm
Friday Jan. 17	AMPLIFY YOUTH GROUP 6:30-8:30 pm
Saturday Jan. 18	*Happy Birthday Judy Osborne*
Sunday Jan. 19 Baby Crying Room available during service in the rear of the Sanctuary Discipleship Classes: Ages: Newborn - 4 5-7 8-12 Teen Adult Children's Church during 2nd service Pre-school 4 & under Ages 5-7 8-12	**8:30 am Service** **10:15 am Sunday School** Adult "Higher Ground" Discipleship Class meets in Fellowship Hall with snacks & refreshments Discipleship Class #3 10:15 in Conference Room with Pastor Dann All other classes in classrooms **11:15 am Service** Gatewatcher Tony Nard